# A B-17 Gunner's Hell in German Skies: Scratch One Rocket Fighter

DOUG BRODIE

ROBERT D. REED PUBLISHERS  •  SAN FRANCISCO, CA

Copyright © 2003 Doug Brodie

All rights reserved. No part of this book may be reproduced without written permission from the publisher or copyright holder, except for a reviewer who may quote brief passages in a review. Nor may any part of this book be reproduced, stored in a retrieval system, or transmitted in any form or by any means electronic, mechanical, photocopying, recording or other, without written permission from the publisher or copyright holder.

Robert D. Reed Publishers
750 La Playa Street, Suite 647
San Francisco, CA 94121
Phone: 650/994-6570 • Fax: -6579
E-mail: 4bobreed@msn.com
www.rdrpublishers.com

Book Design by Marilyn Yasmine Nadel

ISBN: 1-931741-24-7
Library of Congress Card Number: 2002093415
Produced and Printed in the United States of America

S/Sgt E.R. (RALPH) JONES

*B-17 Flying Fortress gunner Ralph Jones*
*compiled a 3-by-5 inch notebook*
*detailing his 35 missions over Germany*
*in just five months, in 1944-45.*

# Dedication

This book is dedicated to all those involved in making possible the establishment and success of the American Air Museum in Britain at the Duxford Royal Air Force Base, England.

# Table of Contents

# *Acknowledgments*

THE AUTHOR WISHES TO THANK the following persons and organizations for their very kind assistance in providing information, photographs and/or technical assistance for inclusion in this publication. Without their help the author would have been unable to produce this book. Jim Watson of Stockton, CA, for his invaluable assistance at the computer; Dr. Neil Young, historian at The Imperial War Museum, London, England; personnel at the American Air Museum in Britain, located at the former Duxford Royal Air Force Base, England; Bomber Command Museum, Hendon, England; T/Sgt Charles W. Pearl of Nantucket, MA; 1st Lt. Henry Konysky of Sherman Oaks, CA; Mrs. Mae Jones of Stockton, CA; Mrs. Henrietta Massie of Jefferson City, MO; Mrs. Dorothy Brodehl of Lockeford, CA; personnel at the U.S. Air Force Historical Research Agency, Maxwell Air Force Base, Alabama; National Geographic Society, Washington, D.C.; personnel at Cesar Chavez Library, Stockton, CA, and especially the late S/Sgt. E.R. (Ralph) Jones of Stockton, CA, without whose written words this book certainly would not exist.

Doug Brodie

# List of Illustrations

# *Aerial Bombardment Missions*

"Oh, Natural" - Fort's Name. My Missions In The E.T.O. As Aerial Gunner On A B-17 Flying Fortress

List Of Raids - E.R. (Ralph) Jones:

Mission No. 1 - Target: Stuttgart, Aug. 14, 1944: Time Flying On Raid - 8 Hours; Below Freezing Temperature - 33 Below; Bomb Load On Mission - Twelve 500-Pounders; Gas Load - 2,780 Gallons

Mission No. 2 - Target - Liepzig, Aug. 16, 1944; 8 1/2 Hours; 30 Below; Five 1,000 Pound Bombs; 2,780 Gallons Of Gas

Mission No. 3 - Kiel Naval Yards, Aug. 30, 1944; 7 1/2 Hours; 35 Below; Five 1,000-Pounders; 2,500 Gallons Of Gas

Mission No. 4 - Mannhiem, Sept. 9, 1944; 7 Hours; 30 Below; Twelve 500-Pounders; 2,500 Gallons

Mission No. 5 - Stuttgart, Sept. 10, 1944; 7 1/2 Hours; 40 Below; Twelve 500-Pounders; 2,500 Gallons

Mission No. 6 - Ruhland, Sept. 12, 1944; 9 1/2 Hours; 45 Below; Ten 500-Pounders; 2,780 Gallons

Mission No. 7 - Holland, Ground Troops - Invasion, Sept. 17, 1944; 6 Hours; 20 Below; Thirty 260-Pounders; 2,000 Gallons

Mission No. 8 - Unna, Germany-Ruhr Valley - Sept. 19, 1944; 7 Hours; 33 Below; Twelve 500-Pounders; 2,100 Gallons

Mission No. 9 - Osnabruck, Sept. 26, 1944; 6 1/2 Hours; 35 Below; Five 1,000-Pounders; 2,300 Gallons

Mission No. 10 - Cologne, Sept. 27, 1944; 6 1/2 Hours; 40 Below; Twelve 500-Pounders; 2,300 Gallons

Mission No. 11 - Magdeburg, Sept. 28, 1944; 8 1/2 Hours; 42 Below; Ten 500-Pounders; 2,780 Gallons

Mission No. 12 - Kassel, Oct. 2, 1944; 8 Hours; 40 Below; Ten 500-Pounders; 2,500 Gallons

Mission No. 13 - Nuremburg, Oct. 4, 1944; 9 Hours; 55 Below; Five 1,000-Pounders; 2,780 Gallons

Mission No. 14 - Cologne, Oct 6, 1944; 6 1/2 Hours; 40 Below; Twelve 500-Pounders; 2,300 Gallons

Mission No. 15 - Schwienfurt, Oct. 9, 1944; 7 1/2 Hours; 43 Below; Ten 500-Pounders; 2,780 Gallons

Mission No. 16 - Cologne, Oct. 15, 1944; 7 1/2 Hours; 40 Below; Fourteen 260-Pounders; 2,500 Gallons

Mission No. 17 - Merseburg, Nov. 2, 1944; 8 Hours; 42 Below; Eighteen 260-Pounders; 2,780 Gallons

Mission No. 18 - Gelserkirchen, (No Date) 1944; 6 1/2 Hours; 50 Below; Chaff (Aluminum Foil); 2,500 Gallons

Mission No. 19 - Battle Front North Of Archen, Nov. 16, 1944; 7 Hours; 38 Below; Thirty 260-Pounders; 2,300 Gallons

Mission No. 20 - Merseburg, Nov. 30, 1944; 9 Hours; 50 Below; Ten 500-Pounders; 2,780 Gallons

Mission No. 21 - Kassel, Dec. 4, 1944; 9 1/2 Hours; 39 Below; Ten 500-Pounders; 2,500 Gallons

Mission No. 22 - Berlin, Dec. 5, 1944; 41 Below; Thirty 260-Pounders; 2,780 Gallons

Mission No. 23 - Merseburg, Dec. 6, 1944; 8 1/2 Hours; 44 Below; Twenty 260-Pounders; 2,780 Gallons

Mission No. 24 - Stuttgart, Dec. 9, 1944; 8 Hours; 58 Below; Twelve 500-Pounders; 2,600 Gallons

Mission No. 25 - Frankfurt, Dec. 10, 1944; 9 Hours; 42 Below; Twelve 500-Pounders; 2,780 Gallons

Mission No. 26 - Merseburg, Dec. 11, 1944; 9 1/2 Hours; 38 Below; Twelve 500-Pounders; 2,780 Gallons

Mission No. 27 - Battlefield In Support Of Ground Troops, Dec. 19, 1944; 7 Hours; 32 Below; Six 1,000-Pounders; 2,600 Gallons

Mission No. 28 - Battlefield In Support Of Ground Troops, Dec. 30, 1944; 7 Hours; 34 Below; Six 1,000-Pounders; 2,600 Gallons

Mission No. 29 - Magdeburg, Jan. 1, 1945; Chaff Run; 9 Hours; 37 Below; 2,780 Gallons

Mission No. 30 - Battle Of The Bulge, Ground Troops, Jan. 3, 1945; 7 Hours; Ten 500-Pounders; 2,780 Gallons

Mission No. 31 - Battle Of The Bulge, Ground Troops, Jan. 5, 1945; 7 1/2 Hours; 36 Below; Twelve 500-Pounders; 2,600 Gallons

Mission No. 32 - Cologne, Jan. 6, 1945; 8 Hours; 47 Below; Three 2,000-Pounders; 2,780 Gallons

Mission No. 33 - Coblenz, Jan. 7, 1945; 8 Hours; 45 Below; Twelve 500-Pounders; 2,780 Gallons

Mission No. 34 - Hit German Troops On The Front Lines Near Cologne, Jan. 10, 1945; 7 1/2 Hours; 60 Below; Thirty-Eight 100-Pounders; 2,600 Gallons

Mission No. 35 - Hit German Troops On The Front Lines, Jan. 13, 1945; 8 Hours; 52 Below; Ten 500-Pounders; 2,600 Gallons

# *Prologue*

THIS IS A STORY BASED UPON the recollections of a World War II Boeing B-17 Flying Fortress machine gunner, Staff Sgt. E.R. (Ralph) Jones. He recalled his experiences in his own descriptive prose after each raid, recording his words in a tiny 3-by-5 inch journal during a five-month period in 1944-45 that saw him complete 35 bombing missions in Europe, most over Germany.

Some episodes he describes also involved a U.S. Army Air Force photographer who, it has been determined through research by the author, flew at least one or more of these same missions and whose work lends credence to our gunner's vivid recollections which he described in his journal as, "Comment on each of my raids over Germany."

As far as can be determined, the two men never met.

Jones' commentary is plain and simple. Samples are included on the following pages. And while gathering information and based upon Jones' descriptions and recollections, an attempt was made to determine whether additional survivors of Jones' original 10-man crew, whom he listed as having also completed 35 missions, were still living 54 years later, in 1999.

Through the assistance of the American Legion Magazine service "Finders-Seekers", Henry Konysky, a co-pilot and later pilot on several of Jones' missions, was located in Sherman Oaks, California.

Another crew member thought by Jones to be a combat casualty and listed in his journal as such, turned out to be very much alive. Konysky said he corresponded regularly with him and that he has continued to live in Nantucket, Massachusetts. He is Charles W. Pearl, then a Tech Sergeant aboard their first Flying Fortress, and he was contacted. Pearl stated the pilot aboard Jones' first bomber, Richard B. Warfel, is also a survivor and continues to reside in Lancaster,

Pennsylvania, where he lived at the time he entered the Air Force during World War II.

T/Sgt Pearl, in recalling events in which he and Jones were involved during aerial combat, described one particular episode that proved intriguing because of its unusual nature, but elusive in the author's attempt to gather information as to whether it actually occurred, and if so, when and where. The event was a claim by Pearl that he and Ralph Jones were credited with shooting down a German rocket fighter plane. Details and photographs are included in the Epilogue.

The author learned of the collection of World War II aerial photographs taken by Gerald R. Massie, the U.S. Army Air Force photographer during the 1944-45 period. Massie died in 1989 and his widow, Henrietta, has his collection of 1,500 photos in her possession. She agreed to allow ten of them to be published on these pages. We know her husband photographed at least one mission in which Jones also participated—a November 2, 1944 raid over Merseburg, Germany, in which 40 Air Force bombers were lost and 14 escort fighters were shot down. The German Luftwaffe lost 130 fighter planes that day out of the 500 sent up to attack the bombers. B-17 gunners shot down 53 of the German fighters and the escort P-47 Thunderbolts and P-51 Mustangs, downed another 77 that cold winter day, according to Jones' journal. Neither he nor Massie received a scratch.

One of Massie's more striking photos was taken that frigid November 2 day in 1944, five miles above Merseburg. A Flying Fortress named "The Blue Streak" was caught in Massie's lens just as it was hit by enemy anti-aircraft fire and burst into flames. Massie wrote on the back of the photo: "The propeller of the engine that has just exploded is in the air in front of the plane."

Mrs. Massie recalled that the following month, December, 1944, her husband wrote home: "Any landing you can walk away from is a good one!"

He explained that a Flying Fortress he had been aboard returning from a raid over Germany had crash-landed and burned at an air base at Bovington, England. Although uninjured, he had lost not only all of his film of action in the skies that day, and cameras and equipment, but six bottles of French perfume he had purchased for his fiancée,

*MAE JONES, (left) widow of E.R. (Ralph) Jones who died in 1974, has assisted in providing his journal for this story. She lives in Stockton, California.*

*MRS. HENRIETTA MASSIE, (right) is the widow of Gerald Massie, a U.S. Army Air Force photographer, who died in 1989. She retains a collection of 1,500 World War II photos, ten of which appear in this book.*

Henrietta Hendrich, now his widow, Henrietta Massie of Jefferson City, Missouri.

Coincidentally, both Jones and Massie served in the same theater of World War II at approximately the same time; both served on the same type of aircraft, the Boeing B-17 Flying Fortress; both survived crash landings uninjured in which their planes were totaled out, and both were on at least one bombing mission together, perhaps more. Both men are deceased and both their widows are living and both have played key roles in making this story possible.

And the author thanks them both.

*FORMING UP* — *These B-17Gs of the 709th Squadron of the
447 Bomber Group were photographed in 1944 forming up over their base
at Rattlesden in Southern England in preparation for a mission over Europe.*
(A BOMBER COMMAND MUSEUM PHOTO, HENDON AIR MUSEUM, ENGLAND)

MISSION NUMBER SIXTEEN [FLEW BALL]

OCT. 15 - 44 [LOST 19 BOMBERS TODAY]

"TARGET"

"COLOGNE GERMANY"

FLAX INTENSE AND ACCURATE,
SAW TWO OF OUR SHIPS
RUN INTO EACH OTHER, NOBODY
GOT OUT, THEN ANOTHER
EXPLODED FROM A DIRECT
HIT, IT LOOKED LIKE
CONFETTI AFTER EXPLOSION,
I SURE AM LOSING LOTS OF
FRIENDS, ONE BOY WENT
DOWN WHO SLEEPS A FEW
BUNKS FROM ME, SURE A
NICE FELLOW, OUR NERVES
ARE SHOT FLIGHT SURGEON
GAVE US A 7 DAY FLAX LEAVE
AFTER THIS ONE (OVER)

---

OCT 16 - 44
FIRST DAY WE WERE GONE
ON OUR FLAX LEAVE, ANOTHER
CREW FLEW OUR SHIP (O-52
NAME OF SHIP "OH! NATURAL"
WAS SHOT DOWN OVER
COLOGNE GERMANY KILLING
ENTIRE CREW, BLEW UP
AFTER WING WAS SHOT OFF
ONE GOOD FRIEND I HAVE FLOWN
WITH ON TWO MISSIONS WAS
ONE OF THEM (POOR KID)
"WE WERE DAM LUCKY"
OCT 29 - 44 T/SGT PEARL ONE
OF MY CREW MEMBERS WAS BUSTED
TO PRIVATE FOR FIRING 3 CLIPS FROM
HIS PISTOL (21 SHOTS) HE WAS TIGHT
HE ALSO WAS GROUNDED FOR A MONTH TOO
THE MAJOR CAUGHT HIM IN THE ACT.

---

MISSION NUMBER TWENTY
NOV. 31 - 44 [FLEW BALL]
TARGET"
MERSEBURG GERMANY
"OIL REFINERY" FLAX WAS
TERRIFIC AND ACCURATE AS
HELL, WE HAD TWO ENGINES
SHOT OUT ANOTHER ONLY
DOING HALF ITS JOB, WE
CAME BACK ALONE OVER GERMANY
DAM LUCKY FIGHTERS DIDN'T
GET US - LANDED AT BRUSSELS
BELGIUM, STAYED AT HOTEL
THERE THAT NIGHT A C-47
TRANSPORT PLANE BROUGHT
US BACK TO ENGLAND, WEATHER
CLOSED IN, WE HAD TO LAND
AT A B-24 BASE (OVER)

---

STAYED ALL NIGHT, CAME
BACK TO OUR BASE THEN,
WE LOST 31 BOMBERS ON
THIS ONE, WE GOT LOBS
OF HOLES IN OUR SHIP
BESIDES THE ENGINES,
THOUGHT WE HAD IT ON
THIS ONE OUR PLANE JUST
DID MAKE BRUSSELS, THIS
TARGET IS SIMPLY HELL
ON EARTH, THEY SALVAGED
THIS PLANE, THIS WAS ITS
LAST MISSION IT REALLY
HAD IT, BRUSSELS IS
SURE INTERESTING AND
A NICE CITY, HOWEVER
THE GERMANS HAD LEFT
THEIR MARK BEFORE WE TOOK IT

*PHOTOGRAPHERS READY — Air Force photographer Gerald R. Massie (left) prepares with three fellow USAAF photographers on a cold November day in 1944 for a mission over Germany in which all four will record the action involving B-17s dropping tons of high explosives in Allied attempts to halt Germany's war production.*

(GERALD R. MASSIE COLLECTION)

# B-17 Memories

A 1932 ARMISTICE DAY EDITORIAL in the prestigious *London Times* advocated abolition of "aerial bombing planes," or at the very least the severe restriction of their use. At the same time the British Admiralty was describing the aerial bombing of any civilian population as "revolting and un-English."

S/Sgt E.R. (Ralph) Jones, age 32, a gunner this 14th day of August, 1944, was assigned to the ball turret in the belly of a United States Army Air Force (USAAF) B-17 Flying Fortress, an "aerial bombing plane," which carried the designation "0-52," and the nickname "OH, NATURAL" painted on her nose. The pseudonym probably was derived from the letter "O" and the addition of the two numerals—five plus two—being seven, referred to in craps, the game of chance, as a "natural," thus "OH, NATURAL."

His plane was high over Nazi Germany's industrial heartland this particular day. Although here he was, a crew-member of an Allied bomber seemingly defying the position taken by the British Admiralty of 23 years previous, Jones probably had never heard of that bombing controversy. Had he known of it, there's little doubt he'd have been in agreement with both the Admiralty's concept and the newspaper's editorial position, but this was a different time and a different place, and this was war.

In light of Ralph's U.S. Army Air Force career, his nickname probably should have been "Lucky."

His wartime career would be compressed into five months, extending from August 14, 1944, through January 13, 1945—five months of pure hell, and probably few airmen in World War II crammed 35 missions into a shorter period of time. Ralph Jones condensed these experiences of flying over and bombing the enemy into a 3-by-5 inch notebook diary which he titled, "*473 hours of flying!*" The exclamation point was his.

1

Expressed in another way, combat time for this gunner, based upon a normal eight-hour workday, 40-hour week, would compare to just short of 12 weeks. And at 32, Ralph wasn't a young kid when he entered the air force. He'd been married a year. His wife, Mae, later said when he returned home he was a "different man" than the one she had married. Their home town was Floydada in the Lone Star State of Texas.

Ralph Jones was considered the "old man" of his outfit, the 305th Bombardment Group, if not his entire Eighth Air Force wing. He was the oldest enlisted man in the group, and he was filling a position probably designed for a younger man—the ball turret assignment. As a result, he experienced some kidney trouble, doubled up in that "ball" from eight to nine-and-a-half hours on round-trip flights deep into Europe. And he did this 20 times until reassignment to waist gunner. Even bundled into a bulky flight suit, his front was "roasting" while his back, up against cold armor plate, would be close to freezing.

The fact that Ralph was even able to return home without a scratch after 35 missions through the most dangerous sky on earth was remarkable—an indication of just how lucky he was. He was quick to admit that God had had a great deal to do with it. Ralph did some serious praying.

For security reasons, he mentioned neither the name nor location of his air base in the tiny journal, other than to indicate it was in southern England. It actually was Chelveston Airdrome in England's midlands, as noted by a former flying mate of Ralph's, contacted by the author in 1999.

Ralph had arrived in England in 1944. It had been two years earlier, in July, 1942, that the USAAF had moved B-17 squadrons into England to begin bombing strategic targets in Europe. At that time the 97th Bombardment Group, flying B-17E models, initially flew raids over France beginning August 17, almost two years to the day before Ralph Jones flew his first mission.

The European strategic bombing campaign officially ended April 16, 1945, two months after Ralph completed his own assignment. The Army Air Force declared its objective completed, but at a high cost: 8,314 bombers lost with 6,378 crews—20,000 airmen killed and another 9,300 wounded.

*CONTRAILS IN THE COLD AIR — Massie observed B-17 contrails resulting from hot engine exhaust hitting 20 to 60 degrees-below-zero air high above German targets and made the scene a thing of beauty, but for German fighter pilots in their fighters, including the new ME 262 jets and ME 163 rockets, the long, white streaks presented targets, and they took advantage of Mother Nature's display by shooting down hundreds of the big bombers.*
(GERALD R. MASSIE COLLECTION)

European Theater target priorities for allied bombers originally had been determined jointly by President Franklin D. Roosevelt and British Prime Minister Winston Churchill at the 1943 Casablanca Conference: submarine construction/maintenance yards; the German aircraft industry; transportation; oil production and finally other targets.

As hostilities progressed, General Dwight D. Eisenhower was placed in command of the coming Allied invasion of France. General Carl A. Spaatz was named commander of the Eighth Air Force. Together, these two generals determined that slightly different priorities would be of greater benefit to the Allies and strategic bombing was concentrated on the German synthetic oil industry, with secondary targets of rail and transportation facilities. This continued from January, 1944, until the end of the war.

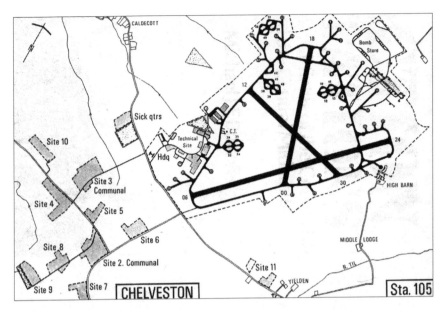

*HOME BASE - Chelveston, from which the "Incredible 305th" Squadron of the Eighth Air Force, flew its missions, was located at Northamptonshire, England. S/Sgt Ralph Jones flew all of his 35 missions from this base.*
(MAP, COPY COURTESY "MIGHTY EIGHTH WAR MANUAL")

Writes Richard G. Davis, a senior historian with the Air Force History Support Office, Bolling Air Force Base, Washington, D.C.: "In the face of determined aerial resistance, the AAF hit synthetic oil on May 12 and 14 (1944). Ultra, (the Anglo-American breaking of high-level German codes) revealed it struck the enemy in the solar plexus. Consequently, Eisenhower made oil strategic air power's top priority for the rest of the war." [1]

Albert Speer, Nazi armaments minister, stated in his post-war memoirs: "(With the beginning, in May 1944, of the Allied attack on oil centers,) a new era in the air war began. It meant the end of German armaments production." [2]

The Allies determined that only denial of oil supplies and systematic blocking of lines of communication could stop the German war machine (since production of aircraft, weapons and vehicles was widely dispersed by 1943) and the main effect of Allied round-the-clock

1.  Richard G. Davis, "Air Force Magazine," November, 2000 "Spaatz," Pages 71-72.
2.  Richard Hallion, "Air Force Magazine," November, 2000 "Airpower, From the Ground Up," Page 41.

*A RACK OF HIGH EXPLOSIVES - American bombers during daylight and British bombers at night carried this type of bomb load on many missions. Some were larger (the largest and heaviest of all conventional bombs was carried by modified British Lancasters—the 22,000-pound H.E. Deep Penetration bomb nicknamed "Grand Slam"), and some were smaller. Jones listed a bomb load of 38 100-pounders, the smallest, on his 34th mission, and three 2,000-pounders, the largest, on mission No. 32 over Cologne.*

(GERALD R. MASSIE COLLECTION)

bombing in raids of up to 1,000 bombers at a time was to keep over a million German soldiers and equipment occupied in home defense.

In the winter of 1942 and spring of 1943, four B-17 groups and a few B-24 Liberator bombers flew raids into Germany in formations of 18 to 21 aircraft, performing well against German fighter planes. As Flying Fortress crews became more experienced, their bombing results began improving. Luftwaffe fighter tactics, however, also improved, including frontal attacks on the B-17s. German anti-aircraft weaponry was also upgraded, bringing down increasing numbers of Allied bombers.

In the winter of 1941-42, shortly after the United States entered World War II, the U.S. and Britain had agreed to undertake combined strategic bombing, which proved successful. It was formed in anticipation of the eventual invasion of mainland Europe.

A total of 127 airfields constructed or commissioned throughout the English countryside for the Royal Air Force were turned over to the USAAF, including Chelveston, located at Northamptonshire in East Anglia. All were designated to handle heavy bombers.

Chelveston was established as a British bomber station in 1940. It was in March, 1942, that the runways were completed and American bombers arrived. U.S. personnel took over the field in July. Nineteen B-17s arrived August 9 and 10. The 305ᵗʰ Bomb Group moved in Dec. 6, 1942 with Col. Curtis LeMay in command through May 18, 1943. (LeMay eventually rose to become a four-star general, and served as U.S. Air Force Chief of Staff from June 30, 1961 - Jan. 31, 1965).

The group began with four squadrons. During this period LeMay experimented with various bombing tactics, losing many bombers during the interim. In January, 1943, several Lockheed Lightning P-38 fighters arrived to assist. On January 27, the 305ᵗʰ joined the 306ᵗʰ Bomb Group with 18 B-17s in the first American attack on Germany.

The 305ᵗʰ became very active following D-Day, June 6, 1944. It had operated as a three-squadron group but following D-Day was combined with the 422nd to operate as a bomber squadron and day bomber raids extended on through the end of the war.

The 305ᵗʰ had the misfortune of being the last B-17 Group to lose a B-17 in action. The 305ᵗʰ had flown 337 raids. General Spaatz arrived in Britain June 18, 1942 and assumed command of the Eighth Air Force. The first mission of American B-17 Flying Fortresses from Britain was a successful 12-bomber operation against a marshalling yard at Sotteville, France, August 17, 1942, just eight months after the U.S. entered the war.

Ralph's very informative diary was kept, after the war, in his wife's possession following his death in 1974.

He noted in his journal that he departed the United States for England July 8, 1944 immediately following graduation from gunnery school and he was assigned to "OH, NATURAL," the B-17 that carried him unscathed through 16 bombing missions before flak and a heavy attack by Luftwaffe fighters blew it out of the sky in a raid over

*JONES' BALL TURRET - Ralph Jones flew 20 of his 35 missions in the ball turret in the under-belly of his B-17. From this position on his bomber he was credited with an "assist" in shooting down an ME 163 rocket fighter, the "KOMET."*

(GERALD R. MASSIE COLLECTION)

Cologne October 16, just two months after Ralph's first raid, August 14. With the bomber went the entire crew of ten.

But fortunately it wasn't Ralph's crew aboard "OH, NATURAL." Perhaps it was that Jones' luck: luck he mentions often in his notebook. It was Mission 17 for the bomber, but Ralph and crew had been granted "flax leave" that day—a chance to rest up.

He writes that on his first 20 missions he was assigned as ball turret gunner which positioned him in the turret in the belly of his B-17, certainly not considered one of the safest assignments in a Flying Fortress. The location did afford him an ideal view of aerial combat around him, the ground warfare raging often several miles below, and the many targets his bomber either hit or passed over, in addition to the flak barrages hurled into the sky around his plane.

The "under," or ball turret was developed early in the Pacific Theater of World War II when it was determined that frontal attacks on Flying Fortresses by Japanese fighter pilots revealed a weakness in the B-17's defensive armament. The early model B-17E's remotely controlled under-turret left much to be desired. Consequently this turret was removed and hand-held guns were often mounted and fired by crew members through the open space where the turret had been located. In some cases the navigator fired these guns.

Within a short time the Sperry under-turret was introduced, and because of its unique shape, it was termed a "ball turret." The machine guns in the "ball" were fixed and it was the entire turret that moved rather than the guns alone. The gunner, Ralph Jones in this case, would sit hunched over between the guns, using a reflector sight which he aimed between his feet. His back would be to the turret entry door.

As ball turret gunner, Ralph remained out of the turret during take-offs and landings. This was in case of an undercarriage failure. He entered the turret once the B-17 was airborne, and each time it was necessary to revolve it to enable the guns to point downward, thus exposing the door, so that Ralph could enter the ball. He often thought the ball turret was not a place for the claustrophobic. It was compact and usually men small in stature were assigned to it. And, owing to the space restrictions, he was unable to wear his parachute. In an emergency he would have to return to the fuselage to obtain his chute and he often wondered what he would do if the wiring controlling the ball was severed by a bullet or flak. Fortunately, that problem never came up and before it could, he was assigned to waist gunner position, but not before he flew four more missions—a total of 20—in the ball.

His B-17's ten-man crew was divided, with four in the forward section of the Fortress. These were officers, with the pilot in the left seat. The co-pilot, navigator and bombardier were also in the nose section. The other six crew members were non-commissioned personnel, with the flight engineer monitoring engine operations, fuel supply, plus miscellaneous duties, and manning the top turret gun. The radio operator doubled as a gunner, manning the gun in the roof of his

*ME 262 NAZI TWIN JET - Allied bombers first encountered Germany's newest aerial threat July 26, 1944. Just two days later the first ME 163 KOMET, Germany's rocket fighter, flew in combat over the Third Reich.*

(HENDON AIR MUSEUM)

compartment. The remaining four men served as gunners in the tail, the ball turret, and the two waist positions.

The B-17G model Flying Fortress, introduced in late 1943 and used through the end of the war, was equipped with chin turrets as an answer to enemy frontal attacks on the big planes. These chin turrets were manned by the bombardier through controls on a column which folded back against the starboard side of the nose as a means of enabling the bombardier to use his bomb sight.

The B-17 was a tough airplane. With the B-24 Liberator, the two were the largest in the U.S. aerial arsenal until the advent of the B-29 Superfortress in the Pacific Theater.

The B-17 bomb load, lighter in comparison with other bombers, such as the B-24 and the British Lancaster, was a subject of some criticism. On occasion, a B-17 would be equipped with under wing racks and would lift operational loads of 12,000 pounds. The B-17F could carry up to 9,600 pounds, composed of six 1,600-pound armor-piercing bombs. Such a load was rarely carried and only on short-range targets.

*A RETURN TO BASE - Following a long 8 to 9 1/2-hour round trip to the heart of Germany,
dodging Hitler's Luftwaffe and managing to evade thousands of anti-aircraft
shells from highly accurate German guns, a tough Flying Fortress would make it
back to base only to collapse on the runway from damage inflicted.
Many a crew was saved because the B-17 was tough.*
(GERALD R MASSIE COLLECTION)

Ralph's records included bomb load totals for all of his 35 missions.
Maximum weight was 7,800 pounds consisting of thirty 260-
pounders, and thirty-eight 100 pounders.

A comparison of bomb load weights for average operational tonnage between the B-17 and the British Lancaster indicates the B-17
averaged four tons while the Lancaster average was ten tons. The B-
17's limiting factor was the size and construction of the bomb bay.
The plane had been designed as a medium bomber and not only did
the bomb bay size limit the overall tonnage carried, but it restricted
individual bombs to the 2,000-pound maximum.

The Eighth Air Force strength during the winter of 1943-44 had
been established at 40 bombing groups of which 21 were equipped

with the B-17 and 19 with the B-24. Several months later five of the Liberator groups were converted to B-17s for a total of 26 B-17 groups. These remained in England until the end of hostilities.

Ralph's first entry in his notebook: "I saw one fighter go down. No chute came out. Flax is lots rougher now that the Germans have moved all of the flax guns they could back into Germany from Holland, Belgium, France, Greece...my heated shoes burned out today. Sure like to froze my feet....it's really Hell, this flax now."

Ralph's spelling of the work "flax," rather than "flak" is his own personal reference to anti-aircraft shrapnel. His reference to his near-frozen feet was a situation not uncommon among bomber crewmen at altitudes of four and five miles in which discomfort was considerable. Heavy clothing needed to ward off the cold impeded movement; frostbite was always a risk if he exposed a bare hand; wearing his oxygen mask, from six to nine hours at a stretch was certainly not pleasant. Long flights under these conditions were fatiguing. A failure in the oxygen supply could quickly cause unconsciousness and often death.

A record of temperature lows during each flight was kept by Ralph and on his first mission that August 14, 1944, it reached 33 degrees below zero. The second mission, August 16, warmed up to 30 below. He comments about more bad "flax" and observes four B-17s going down in flames and only nine parachutes from one of the four. His coldest mission was Number 34 at 60 below over Cologne, Germany.

About Mission Two, he writes: "We lost 23 bombers and three fighters....one of my friends shot down a jet plane (a Messerschmitt ME-262). Good boy. Liepzig is one of the roughest targets in Germany. Our target there was a large synthetic oil refinery. Left it blazing. Flew North Sea going into Germany. I hope and pray we don't get any more like this. Lost lots of friends today." (Ralph will write this often).

The ball turret was very successful in warding off fighter attacks from below but it did present a problem never satisfactorily resolved: shell casings from the twin guns were ejected outside the turret and on occasions caused damage to other bombers in the formation.

While assigned later to the waist gunner position Ralph was still able to view aerial combat activities from a vantage point when he wasn't busy at his guns. After a two-day respite from the second raid, the big bomber greeted the dawn again with a roar, headed this time for the German naval shipyards at Kiel. The sky was filled with friendly cloud formations as the swarm of B-17s, aided by the overcast, dropped their deadly cargo. Ralph again referred to the target as "rough as Hell....gobs of flax guns all sizes. We run the Luftwaffe away....throwed to dam much lead at the dirty B....D."

A synthetic oil refinery at Mannheim was the next target September 9. The crew was fortunate to have had a nine-day rest and was ready for this one. "We got seven holes in our ship. Flax was a solid wall over the target. God was really with us. Germany sure is taking a beating, lots and lots of bomb craters in every city we pass....we lost 23 bombers and four fighters."

Ralph and crew had as their first target that jet fighter plant in Stuttgart when Ralph's feet almost froze. Here they go again. The Allied command is worried about the new ME-262 twin-jet engine fighter and so Mission No. 5 is to destroy that plant in Stuttgart, and according to Ralph's observations, the bombers did exactly that. His words: "We destroyed target!" The underlining and exclamation point were his. This could have been the high point in his Army Air Force career.

The raid took "OH, NATURAL" over France and Holland and through heavy antiaircraft fire which was described as "very close and accurate, bursting right beneath the ball and right in front of our ship." Ralph's description: "barrage flax."

Even though the Eighth Air Force raids, this late in the war, were generally flown with fighter escort—P-47 Thunderbolts, P-51 Mustangs and P-38 Lightnings—heavy losses were still being suffered since Germany was calling in most of its defensive effort to save the fatherland. In reporting on his sixth mission, Ralph writes: "The Luftwaffe was up in strength" as Messerschmitt Bf-109s, Focke-Wulf 190s, an occasional ME-262 jet fighter, and even on several occasions the rare Messerschmitt ME-163 Komet rocket interceptor, appeared in the sky to make life miserable for Allied bombers.

"They were tough, these enemy pilots.....Dam we sure are losing bombers and gobs of friends." This sixth raid is over Ruhland, site of another synthetic oil refinery, and he writes that losses totaled 49 bombers and seven fighters, indicating the mission must have included 500 to 600 bombers, with escort. Temperatures, he notes, were the coldest yet experienced—45 below.

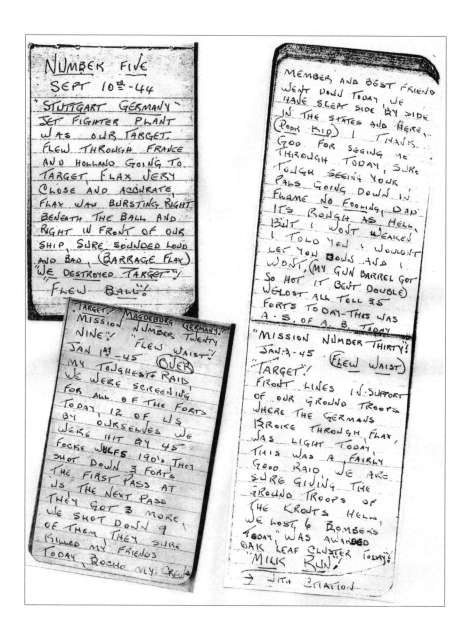

When a B-17 went down it had to have suffered extremely heavy damage or a catastrophic hit. It was described by many of its pilots as a plane that could absorb a tremendous amount of damage and still return home. Ralph, time and again, notes the number of holes punched into his Fortress by enemy bullets and antiaircraft shrapnel.

The B-17's flying qualities were so good it could lose one side of a tailplane or large area of fin and rudder and still return for a safe landing. The bombers often limped home with one or two engines out and damage to hydraulic systems that forced many of those wheels-up belly landings.

Ralph knew the ball turret in such a landing could be a problem. If it was jettisoned and the tail wheel was lowered, airframe damage could be slight and repaired. If the ball remained in place and the tail wheel was not extended, the turret suspension frame usually was forced up through the base of the fuselage. This caused frame distortion and he had observed numerous planes with this type of damage written off as unrepairable.

The main concern in such a situation was that if the ball were to be jettisoned, or if it were to remain, that Ralph not be in it. Of course, he never was.

Mission No. 7, flown September 17, 1944, was an unusual one for Ralph Jones. As he describes it:

"We blasted a path for troops and airborne infantry in the invasion of Holland....one bomber exploded in flames beside us from a direct hit. Another went down close by. Saw some boys get out of this one and their chutes opened. We lost 11 bombers. On the way back we passed the transport planes and gliders on their way for the invasion. We killed Germans by the score and knocked Hell out of our targets....we really saw history in the making. This was the largest airborne invasion in history. Sure glad I was one of the many that helped make this invasion possible. The Krouts were really catching Hell from us."

Weather was an all-important factor in the success or failure of a B-17 mission. The majority of Ralph's flights were made in the fall and winter. Mission No. 8, September 19, 1944, was typical—an ordnance depot at Unna, in Germany's Ruhr Valley. The Flying Fortress took off blind in heavy fog. The weather closed in after the bomber reached its target. The pilot was forced to land at another field in southern England. Forty-three bombers were lost that day. The temperature, Ralph noted, had hit 42 below.

The following mission, No. 9, saw "OH, NATURAL" drop five half-ton bombs on marshalling yards in Osnabruck, Germany, September 26. "A bulls eye!," wrote Ralph. Just 24 hours later,

*ONE LUCKY GUNNER - This isn't Ralph Jones who has just been treated for a superficial back wound, but it could have been. This B-17 gunner made it through the Nov. 2, 1944 Merseburg raid with only a slight wound from German anti-aircraft flak that ripped through his thermal jacket (left) and his parachute (right) that surely saved his life.*

(GERALD R. MASSIE COLLECTION)

September 27, it was Cologne again—a raid he describes as "DAM ROUGH RAID." The big bomber rode through 40 minutes of solid flak. "We lost 20 bombers....lots of my best friends are going down— poor boys."

Mission No. 11, just a night's sleep away, is long—8 1/2 hours— at 45 below. It's Magdeburg in Germany. The crew has just enough time to report in, clean up, catch some sleep, and it's rise and shine.

General Eisenhower and his Supreme Headquarters staff believe they have Germany on the ropes and want to maintain the pressure; hence, round-the-clock bombing, with British Lancasters pasting the Third Reich at night. This time Ralph and crew are aimed at Magdeburg to hit another oil refinery: this one produced one-fifth of the entire output of Germany. On this Ralph has a good friend who has an arm shot off. He writes: "We were hit 6 times by flax."

"Dad," Ralph writes in his journal. "It's tougher than Hell, but I promised you I wouldn't let you down. I am worried lots of times, but Hell, Fred, Glen (Ralph's brother fighting elsewhere in the War) and I can take it. Will tell you some-day (I hope). Lost 49 bombers today. Again, we made the Luftwaffe turn tail and run from our lead."

Kassel, Germany was the target October 11 for Mission No. 12. Ralph's notebook refers to the loss of 16 bombers in this raid; good fighter protection; a tougher Luftwaffe; no holes in the ship (an unusual event), and an Oak Leaf Cluster for his Air Medal. The following mission he refers to as "UNLUCKY MISSION NUMBER THIRTEEN," and it proved to be one of his toughest. The target was Nuremburg, the German city made famous following the war as the site of the International Military Tribunals in which Nazi Germany's surviving leaders were tried for their crimes and convicted as war criminals.

Mission No. 13 required nine long hours of flight time with temperatures of 55 below zero. "OH, NATURAL" again carried five of those thousand-pound bombs. Flights similar to this one, extending for up to nine-and-a-half hours, were being made possible with the addition of wing tanks for the Flying Fortress which increased total built-in tankage from 1,730 gallons to 2,810 gallons. Range was increased from 1,300 miles to 2,200 miles.

At the high altitude operations flown over Europe the extra fuel capacity gave the Fortresses an additional three hours endurance. The

*"ACK - ACK," "FLAK," OR AS RALPH CALLED IT, "FLAX," OR JUST PLAIN "ANTI-AIRCRAFT FIRE" - Whatever it was called, it was deadly. Puffs of black smoke indicate 88 mm and 105 mm shells exploding and spewing metal fragments designed to bring down bombers and kill crewmen. Ralph Jones and Gerald Massie were lucky to fly through these barrages and remain unscathed. Thousands of fliers didn't make it.*

(GERALD R. MASSIE COLLECTION)

tanks acquired the nickname, "Tokyo Tanks" because Pacific Theater Air Force personnel determined they would enable a B-17 to make a one-way trip to Tokyo.

Ralph listed fuel loads carried on every one of his 35 missions. These ranged from a low of 2,000 gallons to a high of 2,810. This much high octane aviation fuel, plus three to four tons of bombs, and thousands of rounds of ammunition, was enough every time a B-17 took off, to make a gigantic ball of fire in the sky should it all go at once....and it often did.

With this in mind, Mission No. 13 "Was a living Hell," as Ralph described it. "Caught flax in France and all over Germany. Saw two Forts go down. (Twenty men) None of those boys got out. We were dam lucky to get back. The flax was so intense and accurate, we were hit 3 times. Don't see how it missed being 300 and us being shot down. We were dam lucky. I am sure tired and my nerves are certainly frayed. WE LOST 32 BOMBERS TODAY."

These were missions with fighter escort toward the end of the war. One publication outlining B-17 operations during this period, (an article with which Ralph Jones would surely have vehemently disagreed) stated that by the summer of 1944 the provision of long-range fighter escort had made attacks by Luftwaffe interceptors on 8th and 15th Air Force bombers "more the exception than the rule." It stated:

"Many B-17 gunners completed their tour of 30 or more combat missions without ever firing their guns in action. By this time factory, modification center and battle zone additions to the B-17, plus the maximum fuel, bomb and ammunition loads and other paraphernalia....led to the reduction in armament in view of the lessened risk of enemy fighter interference."

Jones, on the other hand, was firing his gun to such an extent the "barrel bent double" in one instance because of overheating during combat. In fact, during the five months of his combat experience in the skies over Europe, he makes reference to the loss of 690 Flying Fortresses, which usually carried a crew of ten—a total of 6,900 personnel. Survivors were few. Many of the big bombers went down with all hands aboard.

Mission No. 14, October 4: target—again, Cologne, and this time over one thousand bombers participate through weather so bad "you couldn't see your hand in front of you for 2 hours. We are really catch-

*LOADING 2,000-POUNDERS-USAAF personnel prepare to load one-ton bombs aboard a B-17 Flying Fortress at Chelveston Air Base in preparation for a mission over Europe. Ralph Jones was a gunner in B-17s that carried bombs ranging in size from 100-pounders to these 2,000-pounders. Britain's largest was 11 times this size, a 22,000-pound behemoth, code-named "Grand Slam."*
(A BOMBER COMMAND MUSEUM PHOTO, HENDON AIR MUSEUM)

ing Hell. Hilter (again, Ralph's spelling) and his boys are p'-ng in their pants to. One of the roughest yet!"

The B-17 flew through flak for 29 minutes and was struck by shrapnel 18 times.

Mission No. 15 target was Schweinfurt, October 9. By this time in the war it had become obvious that highly effective antiaircraft weapons with controlling radar had been developed for greater accuracy, to the point that 88mm and 105mm shells could be set to explode at a selected proximity even beyond an altitude of six miles, up where the Flying Fortresses blackened the skies all day, every day. And some targets, such as Schweinfurt, were defended by as many as 300 of these advanced stage guns.

The barrage these formidable weapons threw up was almost unbelievable. Ralph notes that on this raid the bombers hit the heart of the city, with "flax" taking a heavy toll and weather making flying "as dangerous as bullets. But it is an all-out effort with us now, regardless. We lost 33 bombers today. Nice fighter escort. Boy they sure look sweet to us."

Ralph and his crew are unaware that this next mission, No. 16, will be their last in "OH, NATURAL"—B-17 bomber designation number "0-52." Again, the big plane is headed for Cologne and Ralph notes that the flak is intense and he observes two Flying Fortresses collide in mid-air. There are no parachutes.

"Then another exploded from a direct hit. It looked like confetti after the explosion. I sure am losing lots of friends. One boy went down who sleeps a few bunks from me. Sure a nice fellow. Our nerves are shot. Flight surgeon gave us a 7-day flax leave after this one."

Ralph sadly writes: "First day we were gone on our flax leave another crew flew our ship." And at this point he refers to the plane by its number. "0-52 name of ship. 'OH, NATURAL' was shot down over Cologne, Germany, killing entire crew. Blew up after wing was shot off. One good friend I have flown with on two missions was one of them (poor kid). We were dam lucky!"

Ralph and crew returned to duty following their flak leave, but the pressures of combat continued. He writes on October 29 that one of his crew members caves in to the pressure:

"T/Sgt Pearl (Charles W. Pearl of Nantucket, Massachusetts) one of my crew members, was busted to private for firing 3 clips from his

*"BOMBS AWAY" - High over Europe, toward the end of the war B-17s appear shadowy in the dark blue sky, dropping sticks of bombs of various sizes on Nazi targets in an attempt to destroy Germany's ability to manufacture war material such as synthetic oil; a German Messerschmitt ME 262 jet fighter factory, and V-1 buzz bombs and V-2 rockets that were making life miserable for Allied forces, both military and civilian.*
(GERALD R. MASSIE COLLECTION)

pistol (21 shots). He was tight. He also was grounded for a month to. The major caught him in the act."

Ralph doesn't list the name or number of the second bomber to which he and his crew are assigned, now that "OH, NATURAL" has been lost, but he does state the target for Mission No. 17 this November 2 is Merseburg, and the raid results in 40 Allied bombers shot out of the sky. The strike area is the largest oil refinery in the Third Reich, and Ralph's description begins with his oft-repeated phrase, "Flax was Hell. This is the roughest target in Germany. Solid wall of flax and accurate as Hell.

"Our ship jumped all over the skies from explosions of flax all around us. We were dam lucky. Lots of fellows got it on this one. We lost 40 bombers....we only got 4 holes in our ship. I saw 3 men from my Sqn. wounded badly.

"The Krouts sent up 500 fighters at us. Our Fortress gunners shot down 53 of them, our fighter escort shot down 77. Total Krout planes shot down—140. We lost 40 bombers and 14 of our fighter escort. This was rough as they come. We really sweated this one out."

At this point in the war Germany had pulled in fighter planes from all the battle fronts, especially from the Russian lines in the east, in an attempt to halt the ever-increasing bombing of their industrial centers in the heart of Germany.

For the first time Ralph, a few days later, participated in a raid over enemy territory in which his bomber carried no bombs. It was loaded with "chaff"—strips of aluminum foil that was ejected into the air to float down slowly and deflect enemy radar. The target on this raid, Mission No. 18, was an oil refinery in Gelserkirchen. "Very little flax, but dam good thing fighters didn't hit us. We would have been sitting ducks for them. Awarded Oak Leaf Cluster to Air Medal today. Milk run!" Participation November 16 in Mission No. 19 by Ralph and crew helps turn the skies over Germany black with bombers. This is by far the largest raid in which he will participate -1,200 bombers. From his vantage point in the ball turret, he writes:

"Target—Front lines in support of our troops north of Archen. This was the start of the big Winter Offensive. 1,200 Forts took part. We slew Krouts like flies. Knocked out gobs of gun emplacements. The ground troops struck as soon as we left, gaining lots of miles. Also 7 German towns fell. We left the entire battle field ablaze and all of the Germans stunned from the concussion of our bombs. We lost 14 bombers and 5 fighters. Weather was Hell again. We had to land at a R.A.F. base. Our field was completely closed in. We got 13 holes in our ship from flax. It was accurate as Hell. Saw a Fort go down in flames. Saw 4 boys bail out. This was a rough one."

Ralph's final words regarding Mission 19 were trivial in comparison to his description of Mission No. 20, on November 30, which, as it turns out, was his last in the ball turret position. Viewing the scene of battle for the last time underneath, he recounts the hours enroute to Merseburg; the target; the short time over it and his own experiences:

"Oil refinery! Flax was terrific and accurate as Hell. We had two engines shot out. Another only doing half its job. We came back alone over Germany. Dam lucky fighters didn't see us—landed at Brussels, Belgium. Stayed at hotel there that night. A C-47 transport brought us back to England. Weather closed in. We had to land at a B-24 base.

*IN A GERMAN MARSHALLING YARD - When Allied forces sought the assistance of air support as they advanced toward Berlin in late 1944, the intense bombing barrage would often result in destruction beyond belief. It took a tremendous blast to cause this locomotive to stop suddenly and end up standing up.*

(GERALD R. MASSIE COLLECTION)

Stayed all night. Back at our base then. We lost 56 bombers on this one. We got gobs of holes in our ship besides the engines. I thought we had it on this one. Our plane just did make Brussels. This was its last mission. It really had it."

So now, E.R. (Ralph) Jones has literally had two Flying Fortresses shot out from under him and he remains physically unscathed. On his next mission, Number 21, December 4, he is assigned to his new position as a waist gunner. In the latter months of the war this is a somewhat improved assignment in a B-17 over that of earlier models.

During operational missions the previous year the waist positions were open, resulting in gunners in the rear of the plane being exposed to the icy blast of the slipstream. A second problem was that of location of the two side gunners. They often bumped each other as they swung from side to side, aiming and firing at attacking enemy aircraft. This would occasionally dislodge one or the other's oxygen connection, resulting in serious consequences.

The solution to this problem was to move the starboard waist gunner position forward, thus allowing both gunners more freedom of movement. In early 1944, Plexiglas coverings were installed during production of the B-17, and modifications were made in combat areas to install a framed cover at the waist gunner position.

Mission 21 he describes as a "Milk Run." The target is Kassel, Germany, a marshalling yard. It does turn out to be his longest, however—9 1/2 hours. Other Flying Fortresses involved are not so fortunate. Ten are shot down.

Mission No. 22 target is Berlin, December 5. The crew hardly has time to rest, change and eat. On this raid Ralph says he loses "nine good friends. Sure lots of fellows wounded. We lost 12 bombers and several of our fighters. The Krouts lost 90 fighter planes today....the Luftwaffe is getting Hell kicked out of them when they come up."

Top speed for a B-17G was officially listed as 278 miles per hour, but top speeds meant very little when it came to combat performance of the Flying Fortress. The type of operation often involved flying formations in which a specified cruising speed was required. This would vary from 165 to 180 miles per hour.

Modifications in the planes were constantly being made and might depend upon the opposition encountered; improvements in systems, such as changing from hydraulic to electrically-operated turbo-super-

*WAIST GUNNERS - Ralph Jones flew his final 15 missions as a Flying Fortress waist gunner. Two waist gunners worked at opposite sides of the bomber. Quarters were cramped, but they shot down many attacking German fighters. Ralph's 50-caliber gun got so hot it "bent double" on his 29th mission over Magdeburg, Germany.*
(A BOMBER COMMAND MUSEUM PHOTO, HENDON AIR MUSEUM)

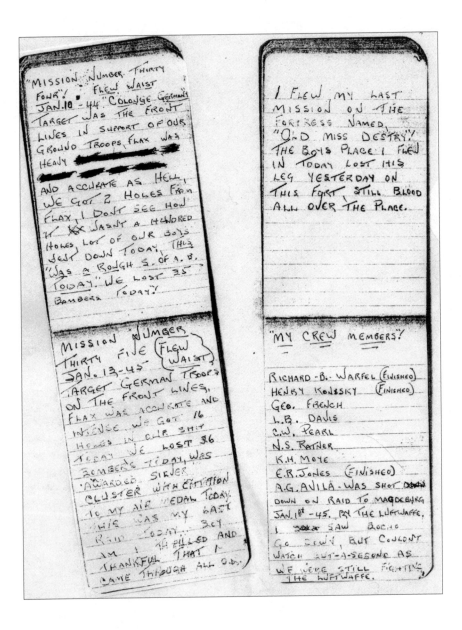

"MISSION NUMBER THIRTY FOUR", FLEW WAIST. JAN. 10 - 44. COLOGNE GERMANY WAS THE FRONT TARGET LINES IN SUPPORT OF OUR GROUND TROOPS, FLAX WAS HEAVY ~~~~~~~~~~ AND ACCURATE AS HELL, WE GOT 2 HOLES FROM FLAX, I DON'T SEE HOW IT WASN'T A HUNDRED HOLES, LOT OF OUR BOYS WENT DOWN TODAY, THIS "WAS A ROUGH S. OF A. B. TODAY." WE LOST 35 BOMBERS TODAY.

MISSION NUMBER THIRTY FIVE (FLEW WAIST) JAN. 13-45, TARGET GERMAN TROOPS ON THE FRONT LINES, FLAX WAS ACCURATE AND INTENSE WE GOT 16 HOLES IN OUR SHIP TODAY, WE LOST 36 BOMBERS TODAY, WAS AWARDED SILVER CLUSTER WITH CITATION TO MY AIR MEDAL TODAY. THIS WAS MY LAST RAID TODAY, BOY AM I THRILLED AND THANKFUL THAT I CAME THROUGH ALL O.K.

I FLEW MY LAST MISSION ON THE FORTRESS NAMED, "OLD MISS DESTRY", THE BOYS PLANE I FLEW IN TODAY LOST HIS LEG YESTERDAY ON THIS FORT, STILL BLOOD ALL OVER THE PLACE.

"MY CREW MEMBERS!"

RICHARD - B. WARFEL (FINISHED)
HENRY KONSSKY (FINISHED)
GEO. FRENCH
L.B. DAVIS
C.W. PEARL
N.S. RATNER
K.H. MOYE
E.R. JONES (FINISHED)
A.G. AVILA - WAS SHOT DOWN DOWN ON RAID TO MAGDEBURG JAN. 1st - 45. BY THE LUFTWAFFE, I SAW BOCHO GO DOWN, BUT COULDN'T WATCH BUT-A-SESONE AS WE WERE STILL FIGHTING THE LUFTWAFFE.

charger regulators; types of armament; improved radar; improved engines, and many others. On Mission No. 23 it's a similar story - catch a few winks; change clothes, grab a bite to eat, and it's December 8....with the target, that dreaded place, Merseburg.

"Flax is Hell as usual. We only got three holes in our ship from flax today. We were dam lucky. We flew lead, the most dangerous spot there is in a formation. I hope and pray God we knocked this target out. A man can't keep going there and come back safely. We lost 4 bombers and 4 fighters. This was our lucky day, just losing this many Forts at this target was extra lucky 'No fooling!' We made the Luftwaffe keep its distance today (good show). 'They don't care for our slugs'."

By Ralph's figures, the big bomber dropped twenty 160-pounders on Merseburg during this raid and he and the crew got a breather.

It was not until December 9 that they pulled duty again—two full days between missions. And the next one, Number 24, was another marshalling yard, this time in Stuttgart. His plane was hit four times by flak and four Fortresses were shot down.

The Stuttgart raid was described as "Not to bad. This was my 3rd raid on this target....fairly rough, but not quite as bad as the times before." But, hello again, it's back to Frankfurt for Mission No. 25, just a day later, December 10. He writes, "We caught them asleep this time. This is always a rough target. The other groups caught Hell behind us. We were just lucky, that's all. No bombers lost today. This is the way we like them," and he added, "Milk run."

Hated Merseburg pops up again as Mission No. 26 target, December 11, and it's the oil refinery again. "This is 4 times for me to this Hell hole. We lost 19 bombers and 9 fighters. 'The Luftwaffe came up!'"

At this point in his little notebook Ralph writes a short prayer: "Please, God, don't let them send me to this place again," adding, "10 holes today."

God was listening. Ralph flew nine more missions, none to Merseburg.

Safety countermeasures were constantly being tried and experimented with Army Air Force personnel and plane manufacturers as a means of providing flying crews protection against flak and bullets from attacking fighter planes. These included frequent bomber formation deviations in course and altitude and installation of armor plate. Changes in the form of opposition would result in changes in countermeasures. At one point much of the B-17 armor plate was removed at crew positions and so-called "flak curtains" substituted. These consisted of a series of laminated plates in canvas designed to check low velocity shell splinters.

Such protective devices probably saved the lives of many bomber crew members, and Ralph very well could have been on of those lucky ones.

Christmas, 1944, and Ralph was able to celebrate it at his base rather than on a mission. In fact it was not until four days later, on December 29, that he flew Mission No. 27, and this was in support of ground troops at the "Battle of the Bulge"—the Battle of the Ardennes, when a German offensive created a "bulge" in the front line of the Allied invasion. This necessitated the temporary diversion of all available heavy bomber units to attack assembly points and communication centers within and behind the bulge. The Allied forces were successful in staving off the Nazi push and a general blitz on transport in Germany followed in February, 1945.

"Support of our ground troops where the Germans broke through. We really gave the Huns Hell. We were so glad to help our boys out (flax light). 'Milk Run!' for us. Very thankful. We lost 12 Forts."

Although heavy defensive armament was provided B-17s, it became evident that without fighter escort the bombers were highly vulnerable to enemy fighter attack with heavy casualties as a result. Royal Air Force short-range Spitfire escorts were replaced in the spring of 1943 by U.S. P-47s. Losses were reduced until daylight raids were increased and began to outdistance the Thunderbolts. At the same time Luftwaffe defenses improved and B-17 losses again were on the increase.

In a raid on Schweinfurt October 13, 1943, sixty B-17s were lost out of 291 planes—a loss ratio of 20 per cent. The situation was remedied only after the introduction of the P-51 Mustang fighter interceptor. These were able to escort the bombers all the way to the target. They fought on level terms with the German defenders.

Mission No. 28 for Ralph was a repeat in assisting at the Battle of the Bulge, this time with eight bombers going down. "Flax wasn't to bad. We had a pretty good raid today (About Time.) MILK RUN."

*RALPH JONES AND GERALD MASSIE ON SAME MISSION NOV. 2, 1944 - This is Ralph's first of four missions over Merseburg, site of the largest oil refinery in the Third Reich. Massie caught this Flying Fortress called "The Blue Streak" on film just after it was hit by flak—German anti-aircraft shells. A string of eighteen 260-pound bombs has just been released by a bomber above, right. Massie wrote a note on this photo: "The propeller of the engine that has just exploded is in the air in front of the plane."*
(GERALD R. MASSIE COLLECTION)

*DEADLY ME 163 ROCKET FIGHTER - This artist's rendition of Nazi Germany's "KOMET" shows it at its deadliest. The pilot has shut off his power at 600 mph and is about to attack a B-17 Flying Fortress at 29,000 feet over Merseburg. This illustration graces the cover of British author Jeffrey L. Ethell's book, "KOMET: The Messerschmitt 163."*

Ralph and crew didn't know it, but their next mission, No. 29, was flown on the first day of the final year of World War II—New Year's Day, January 1, 1945—and he described it as "My toughest raid." The target was Magdeburg, Germany, and half of his flight is lost—six out of twelve Fortresses—"a chaff run."

"We were screening for all the Forts today, 12 of us. By Ourselves. We were hit by 45 Focke Wulf 190s. They shot down 3 Forts the first pass at us. The next pass they got 3 more. We shot down 9 of them. They sure killed my friends. Today Bocho, crew member and best friend went down. (This was A.G. Avila of Brilliant, New Mexico). I saw Bocho go down, but couldn't watch but a second as we were still fighting the Luftwaffe. We slept side by side in the States and here, (poor kid). I thank God for seeing me through today. Sure tough seeing your pals going down in flame."

Ralph then pens another note to his father in his little notebook: "No fooling, Dad, it's rough as Hell, but I won't weaken. I told you I wouldn't let you down and I won't."

An indication of the pressures on this B-17 gunner, firing from the waist position, is this entry in his tiny journal: "My gun barrel got so hot it bent double....We lost all toll 35 Forts today....this was a S. of a B." (The underlining is Ralph's in this case he obviously was firing at the attacking Focke Wulf 190s).

Two days later, January 3, Ralph is back in the air headed again for the Battle of the Bulge: "Target! Front lines in support of our ground troops where the Germans broke through." He notes flak is light; the group lost six bombers, and he was awarded an Oak Leaf Cluster. He describes the raid as "MILK RUN."

He adds a notation: "With citation," referring to his medal.

A statement from U.S. Army General Omar Bradley was made later in 1945 with regard to the work the Army Air Force bombers were doing: "From the high command to the soldier in the field, German opinion has been agreed that airpower was the most striking aspect of Allied superiority."[3]

Mission No. 31, January 5, 1945, is a duplicate of the previous raid at the Battle of the Bulge, with another 13 bombers downed. "Fairly good raid for us," writes Ralph. "This weather is Hell now to fly in."

Mission No. 32 the following day, January 6, is another raid over Cologne in which 17 more Flying Fortresses are lost to enemy fire. He again writes: "My nerves are just about completely shot," and adds that the ground crew counted seven holes from flak. These were patched up during the night and his bomber was back in the air the next morning for Mission No. 33, January 7. The target is Coblenz, Germany, to hit marshalling yards, "supplying the front line Krouts where the Huns broke through. Flax was accurate today. 4 boys wounded today from it. We lost 18 bombers today. We got 8 holes today."

January continues to be a busy month. For the fifth time in just nine days Ralph is back in the sky, headed again for Cologne, the same city over which his first bomber, "OH, NATURAL," met its fate.

3. (Ibid), Page 41.

There's little doubt this fact entered Ralph's mind as he sees the city below. He even makes a mistake in his little journal by referring to the date as "Jan. 10-44" instead of 1945.

"Flax was heavy and accurate as Hell. We got 2 holes....don't see how it wasn't a hundred holes. Lot of our boys went down today. This was a rough S. of a B. We lost 35 bombers," indicating the raid consisted of at least 500 or more planes.

That number "35" was of importance the following day, too. As Ralph explains it:

"Mission number thirty-five-Jan. 13 (Flew Waist). Target German troops on the front lines. Flax was accurate and intense. We got 16 holes in our ship today. We lost 36 bombers today. Was awarded silver cluster with citation to my Air Medal today. This was my last raid today. Boy am I thrilled and thankful that I came through all OK. I flew my last mission on the Fortress named 'Old Miss Destry!' The boy's place I flew in today lost his leg yesterday on this Fort. Still blood all over the place."

Field Marshal Gerd von Rundstedt, the commander of the attack at the Bulge, stated that the main reason for the failure of the Ardennes Offensive was his own lack of fighters and reconnaissance planes and the tremendous tactical airpower of the Allies, according to U.S. General Omar Bradley in 1945.[4]

Ralph listed his original crew members. Of this group of ten, only he and three others survived the five months tour of duty. The six casualties were Flight Officer George H. French, 22, bombardier, of Mount Vernon, NY; 2nd Lt. Louis B. Davis, 22, navigator, of St. Joseph, MO; S/Sgt Ned S. Ratner, 20, tail gunner, of Houston, TX; T/Sgt K.H. Moye, 22, radio operator (no address); G.T. Littleton of San Antonio, TX, and his close buddy, T/Sgt Ambrosio Gonsales (Bocho) Avila, 22, waist gunner, of Brilliant, NM.

The four survivors were Ralph; First Lt. Richard B. Warfel, 20, pilot, of Lancaster, PA; Second Lt. Henry Konysky, 26, co-pilot, of Sherman Oaks, CA, and T/Sgt Charles W. Pearl, 19, of Nantucket, Massachusetts.

Ralph writes in his notebook, just seven months after arriving in Belfast, Northern Ireland:

4. (Ibid), Page 41.

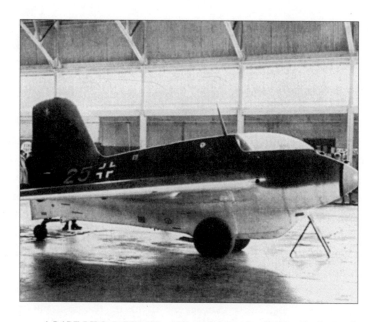

*A RARE BIRD DOWNED - S/Sgt Ralph Jones and T/Sgt Charles Pearl,
both gunners aboard B-17 "OH, NATURAL" were credited in the fall of
1944 with shooting down a Messerschmitt ME 163 "KOMET" rocket-
powered interceptor-fighter, such as this one.*
(JOHN A. TAYLOR PHOTO)

"Left E.T.O. (European Theater of Operations) Feb. 5, 1945. Left
Scotland on the Queen Mary, the largest luxury liner afloat (84,000
dreadnaught tons). We landed New York Feb. 11 - 45."

S/Sgt E.R. (Ralph) Jones spent five months in Hell, and he
returned, unscathed physically, to tell about it in the form of his tiny
3-by-5 inch journal.

Perhaps he thought, after returning to the U.S. that with less than
six months in Europe he might be sent to the other side of the world,
to continue fighting in the Pacific. Near the end of his notebook he
made an entry:

"PACIFIC?"

But he wasn't. Ralph had finished his war.

At approximately the time Ralph and T/Sgt Pearl were ending their tour of duty, Nazi Propaganda Minister Joseph Goebbels, wrote three entries in his diary:

March 12, 1945: "The morale of the German people, both at home and at the front, is sinking ever lower. The Reich propaganda agencies are complaining very noticeably about this. The people think that (they are) facing a perfectly hopeless situation in this war. Criticism of our war strategy does not now stop short even of the Fuhrer himself....The people will continue to do their duty and the front-line soldier will defend himself as far as he has a possibility of doing so. These possibilities are becoming increasingly limited, however, primarily owing to the enemy's air superiority....The total paralysis in west Germany also contributes to the mood of increasing pessimism among the German people."

In a March 15, 1945 diary entry, Goebbels wrote: "Not only our military reverses but also the severe drop in the German people's morale, neither of which can now be overlooked, are primarily due to the unrestricted enemy air superiority."

Goebbels, reflecting on a conversation with Hitler, on March 21, 1945, wrote: "Again and again we return to the starting point of our conversation. Our whole military predicament is due to enemy air superiority." [5]

5. (Ibid), Page 41-42.

# *Epilogue*

WHEN CONTACTED BY THE AUTHOR at his home in Sherman Oaks, California in January, 1999, Henry Konysky recalled his assignment with the 305th Bombardment Group in 1944 and 1945. As a 2nd Lieutenant, he flew his first two flights in August, 1944, as co-pilot in B-17 Flying Fortress 0-52—"OH, NATURAL," with 1st Lt. Warfel as pilot and Ralph Jones as ball turret gunner.

Konysky specifically recalled a January 1, 1945 New Year's Day mission over Magdeburg, Germany, in which his group of twelve fortresses was flying lead, screening for a bombing run....as Ralph described the flight: "By ourselves."

Konysky recalled the raid: "I think we were carrying chaff. I saw these fighters coming at us and I thought, 'Oh great. They're fighter support'....they looked at first like P-47 Thunderbolts with that flat nose....but as they closed in, what appeared at first to be P-47s turned out to be German Focke Wulf 190s and they shot down half our group."

Ralph's description of the same raid, his 29th, was nearly identical, and he described it as, "My toughest."

As a pilot, Konysky must have done some fancy flying that day, with some of that Jones' luck. Whether he and Jones were aboard the same B-17 could not be determined.

Konysky said he has corresponded with T/Sgt C.W. Pearl of Nantucket, Massachusetts, since their flying days in World War II. Supplied with Konysky's information about Pearl, the author contacted him in March, 1999. Pearl said he returned to his home town of Nantucket following his discharge from the Air Force and taught school there until his retirement. He has kept in touch not only with Konysky, but with Warfel whom he said continues to live in Lancaster, PA.

While in the Air Force, Pearl served as a flight engineer and was the enlisted "boss" of his B-17 crew. He recalled the flight crew members as those listed by Ralph. As flight engineer, Pearl also was top turret gunner. He added that eventually a tenth crew member, a waist gunner, was dropped from the roster and that the crew then served with just nine members. This was due, he said, to the heavy casualties suffered by the bomber command during that period.

"One of my duties was to keep the actual roster of the men flying each trip. I know this list for ever! Rarely did the whole (original) crew fly together regularly."

Pearl said he, Warfel, Konysky and Davis usually flew together as a "lead" crew, in addition to any "spares" or volunteers, who might elect to join them as "lead."

When contacted in 1999 at his Nantucket home, Pearl described the bombers in which he served as top turret or tail gunner/observer as the "B-17G" model, the model that served until the War's end.

"Our crew was 'unusual'. The pilot and navigator were super good, and went out for lead crew after apprenticeship. Co-pilot went out for pilot. Bombardier was kind of a zero. Jones was an 'old man' at 32 years of age. He was the oldest enlisted man in 305 GRP, if not in the flying wing....I was a good guy. Our pilot wanted me in his crew as he became lead crew. Plus I was in the hospital with pneumonia one time. Also lost my stripes and was off flight duty for 'promiscuous use of firearm' for (all of) Nov. 1944.

"I also kept a secret diary. At a reunion one time I loaned it out and never never got it back.

"I do know that I/we started bombing Aug. 14, 44, and I ended my 35 (missions) 'tour' on March 15, 1945. (His European tour of duty was longer than Ralph's because of the pneumonia and the firearm incident in which he was grounded for a month). I shipped home from Liverpool on the day F.D.R. (President Roosevelt) died. I went to Berlin 3 times; to Cologne 5 times; to Nuremburg 3 days in a row. To Holland once with frag. bombs at low altitude 8000 ft to disable big bridges."

An unusual incident was described by Pearl when asked whether he or Jones ever shot down an enemy plane, since Jones never mentions a "kill" in his journal. Pearl replied that he and Ralph did share official credit for shooting down a German rocket fighter plane, the

# ENCOUNTERS WITH JET AIRCRAFT

## Both Bombers and Fighters Met Me-163s
## On 16 August, and P-51s Destroyed Two

COMBAT with jet-propelled aircraft encountered by the first and second forces of Eighth Air Force bombers and fighters on 16 August resulted in claims of 2-0-1 for fighters and provided further clues to the tactics and maneuverability of these aircraft in combat.

Two out of six Me-163s attacked the high group of a combat wing of B-17s near Bohlen ; the enemy aircraft made two passes, the first from 11 o'clock high, after which they turned and came back on the tail of the formation from about 2,000 feet above. They came in with jets off and fired from cannon in their wings. When they had approached to within 200 yards, they would turn on jets and break away so fast that, according to crews, it was impossible to trace them. Yet a straggling B-17 of the first combat wing of this force, which was attacked by a single Me-163 about five miles west of Kothen, successfully evaded it.

The claims of 2-0-1 were netted in the Gotha area, when a P-51 group engaged four jet-propelled aircraft. The following is a full report on the encounters :

At 1045, Col. M—— and his wingman, Lt. J——, were headed west at 27,000 feet at Bad Lausich (south of Grimma, southeast of Leipzig) at 5 o'clock position on three B-17 boxes flying 26-27,000 two miles away. Col. M—— saw a long, dense, white contrail, half a mile long, obviously non-atmospheric, climbing at great speed toward the last box of bombers. The contrail was first seen at 27,000 feet, headed northwest, and was unmistakable for the trail of a rocket-ship because of its speed ("climbing faster than airplanes cruise straight and level").

Col. M—— saw only one contrail. It came in at a distance of two miles on the bombers from 8 o'clock, climbed to 28,000 feet and cut out about 400 yards from the bombers. Colonel M——, on the wrong side of the bombers, realized he could not intervene. He saw a straggling B-17 at 25,000 feet two miles away and two miles to the right of the bomber box under attack. M—— decided the enemy aircraft would select this as a target and accordingly dove at once for the straggler.

The single enemy aircraft came through the bomber box and headed for the straggler, with no jet visible. Although M—— had begun his dive at once and had two miles to cover, the Jettie travelled more than a mile to the bombers, went through them and covered two more miles to the straggler, reaching it before M—— and his wingman arrived. These two were clocking more than 400 IAS at 25,000 feet. The Jettie overshot the straggler and began to

flatten out, losing 1,000 feet of altitude. M—— caught him half a mile from the straggler at about 23,000 feet and opened fire at 1,000 feet, 15-degree deflection, closing to zero feet and getting strikes on the tail and left side of the fuselage. He overshot and pulled off steeply to the left. J—— was 1,000 feet behind the Colonel and came in slightly below the Jettie, at an angle of 10 degrees to the right. He opened fire at 1,000 feet. The enemy aircraft flipped on his back and began to split-ess. J—— allowed three radii, saw no strikes and, at a 60-degree angle, increased his lead. He saw multiple strikes on the top of the canopy. He then hit the enemy aircraft's wash, blacked out and recovered at 14,000 feet. He claims this plane destroyed, and says it looked like the published Me-163 drawing, except that its tail was bigger and stubbier.

Colonel M——, however, describes the plane as "more like a flying wing than the published drawing, with a very blunt nose, sharp dihedral on sweptback mainplane, no horizontal tail-plane, an extremely thick tail, stubby ; about one-third the size of a B-17 in span, and much bigger than a P-47."

Colonel M—— pulled out of his climbing turn to the left and saw J—— off to the right, going down, and another Jettie circling off to the left. It is possible this was the original Jettie attacked, but this is believed improbable because that one was going straight down when last seen. The new Jettie was a mile from Colonel M—— and 5,000 feet below his altitude of 24,000 feet. It was in a spiralling slight turn, down and to the left, with plenty of speed. M—— peeled off, diving at and slightly in front

*continued on next page*

*SECRET AIR FORCE ROCKET
FIGHTER REPORT -
Information regarding Germany's new and
unique rocket fighter-interceptor, the
Messerschmitt ME 163 "KOMET" was
in the "secret" category during 1944-45,
when this combat narrative of August
16, 1944, was distributed to fighter and
bomber wings. Eighth Air Force
P-51 Mustangs destroyed two of the rocket
planes that day.*

of the enemy aircraft. He closed at 400 IAS in a 30 degree dive while the enemy aircraft made two turns, and came in on the left, inside the enemy aircraft circle, opening fire at 10 degrees, 700 feet, and closed to 100 feet. He stayed inside the turn with ease and maintained it for 5 to 10 seconds before overshooting. Hits on the left side of the enemy aircraft's rear fuselage caused an explosion "about as big as the whole tail," and the left rear fuselage came off from the cockpit back. The enemy aircraft flopped down in a spiral "like a dead bomber."

When J—— saw Colonel M—— start for the straggler, he also saw three dense half-mile long contrails, white, at great speed, approaching the middle box of bombers. He thought at first it was rocket flak, or smoke bombs. Then the contrails went through and above the bombers at a very steep angle and abruptly ended.

After Colonel M——'s enemy aircraft exploded, he saw another Jettie, jet off, a mile east (8,000 feet) circling at his altitude. He was low on gas and did not engage.

Fifteen minutes after Colonel M—— first called in the jet-propelled aircraft, Captain H—— and Lt. S——, at 27,000 feet, south east of Zwenkau (south of Leipzig), saw at a range of 10-12 miles a well-molded bleached white jet, very thick, going straight up from 25,000 feet in what turned out to be an Immelman, breaking at 32,000 feet, when the jet petered off as the enemy aircraft headed down again.

The enemy aircraft, over the center of Leipzig, obviously was flying at great speed, about 300 m.p.h. going straight up. H——, short of gas, continued home. S—— turned back to the northeast, hoping to intercept the enemy aircraft's southeast course. A box of B-17 bombers at 25,000 feet was five miles to S——'s right rear, and when he came up to it, same altitude, he saw the Jettie attacking from the bombers' starboard (north) side.

The enemy aircraft was two miles from the bombers, level, and attacking from 3 o'clock. S—— was at 2 o'clock on the enemy aircraft. He closed and opened fire from 500 yards. The enemy aircraft fired one burst from a protruding weapon, mounted on its port wing. This weapon, later seen from 50 feet, looked like a single cannon, protruding two feet, from the port wing only, none being seen on the starboard wing.

S—— chandelled up and to the left and the enemy aircraft turned to the left, away from the bombers, so that S—— came out at 300 IAS. He thought the enemy aircraft was going faster than he, and opened fire at 1/2 radii lead. He then saw he was overtaking the enemy aircraft very rapidly and dropped all flaps, trying to hold his position, but overshot, seeing no strikes. He skidded up and to the right, losing speed, and the enemy aircraft pulled up and to the left. S—— turned down and to the left sharply. He could not see the enemy aircraft and used 20-degree flaps to make one turn, and then saw the enemy aircraft off his left wing at 300 yards range and the same level (8,500 feet). The enemy aircraft used two short bursts of his jet to get away, climbing slightly. S——, at 50 to 60 degrees on the enemy aircraft, gave him six-plus radii, and fired from 300 to 400 yards, getting strikes on the right wing. The enemy aircraft turned on his jet and dove away at great speed. He levelled out on the deck.

S—— agrees with J—— that this enemy aircraft is very accurately pictured in the Me-163 illustration. He agrees with Colonel M—— that the enemy aircraft were black or a very ugly brown, unwaxed. S—— thinks that when he overran the enemy aircraft it was down to 150 m.p.h. straight and level. Neither Col. M—— nor Lt. S—— can quite account for the loss of altitude to 8,000 feet, of which they are positive. Both M——'s aircraft had German crosses on the upper wing surfaces. S—— saw no markings

⊂∗⊃

# Supersonic Wind Tunnel at Peenemünde Described

DESCRIPTION of a supersonic wind tunnel, in which airspeeds exceeding three times the speed of sound were developed, has been provided by a German prisoner who was employed for some time at Peenemünde.

This wind tunnel was used by the *Aerodynamische Abteilung* of the German Army section of Peenemünde—the *Waprüf* 11 department of the War Office, located at Peenemünde East. (The GAF occupies Peenemünde West.)

The terrific air speeds were achieved by connecting the wind tunnel to a large vacuum chamber, according to the prisoner. This chamber was a steel sphere some 25 meters (82 feet) in diameter. When air was exhausted from this, the flow could be introduced

through the tunnel by the opening of a valve, at a rate which could be basically determined by the extent of the vacuum created in the chamber. Fine adjustment of airflow and pressure could be achieved by inserting the desired pairs of venturi-shaped blocks, selected from a number of sets of varying dimensions, and by the manual adjustment of a pair of diffuser vanes.

Tests on scale models of such projectiles as the FX radio-controlled bomb, flak shells, and "secret weapons" of the rocket type were conducted in the tunnel. Under supersonic speed conditions, these normally lasted only 10 to 15 seconds, as compared with as much as 24 hours sometimes involved for subsonic speeds.

*PILOT CLIMBS ABOARD GERMAN ROCKET PLANE - He wears a combination smock manufactured from acid-proof material as protection against the (T-Staff) rocket fuel.*
(PHOTO COURTESY WILLIAM GREEN,
AUTHOR "ROCKET PLANES OF THE THIRD REICH")

Messerschmitt ME 163 "Komet," determined by experts to be the most dangerous production aircraft ever built. An estimated 370 came off Third Reich assembly lines between April, 1943 and February, 1945.

## THE MESSERSCHMITT ME 163 KOMET

Because of its unusual place in aerial warfare history, and the little publicity it received, the author researched the Komet and included the following narrative as a fitting conclusion to the Ralph Jones' story.

During its early development it was known officially as the "Komet," but was also nicknamed by the Germans as "Die Motte"—in English, "The Moth," and Eighth Air Force fighter pilots referred to it as "The Swallow." One pilot's narrative noted in an Air Force report:

"...The first operational use by the enemy of jet-propelled (rocket) fighters, five Me-163 Swallows being seen near (and driven off from) the bombers on the Merseburg show of 28 July (1944) (just two weeks before Ralph Jones arrived in Europe) as Colonel Avalin P. Tacon's widely-circulated teletype special report, appended, duly narrates." (A message referring to the first ME 163 encounter, including a description of the plane and a warning as to its dangerous possibilities).

Through the American Air Museum, located at the former World War II Royal Air Force Base at Duxford, England, the author was able to make contact with Dr. Neil Young, historian at London's Imperial War Museum. As a result, references were drawn from the following publications as supplied by Dr. Young:

"*The Last Year of the Luftwaffe: May 1944 to May 1945*" by Alfred Price; "*The Warplanes of the Third Reich*" by William Green; "*The Incredible 305th—the 'Can Do' Bombers of the 305th*" by Wilbur H. Morrison; "*Komet; the Messerschmitt ME-163*" by Jeffrey L. Ethell; "*Action stations: Military Airfields of the Cotsworlds and the Central Midlands*" by Michael J.F. Bowyer, and "*Mighty Eighth War Manual*" by Roger A. Freeman.

In addition, microfilm files containing World War II narratives by Eighth Air Force fighter pilots and bomber crew members were obtained from the U.S. Air Force Historical Research Agency, Maxwell Air Force Base, Alabama. After many years in the Agency's files, these were declassified from their original "Secret" and "Confidential" status.

The Eighth Air Force, from mid-1944 on through the end of World War II, had to face two new aerial foes, previously unseen and unmet by Allied planes in "that sky over Germany." They consisted of a twin-jet-powered fighter-bomber and a rocket-powered fighter-interceptor.

All Allied aircraft, and all other Nazi aircraft, throughout the War, were piston engine, propeller-driven (with the exception of the jet-powered British Gloster Meteor, which operated on a very limited basis in 1944 and 1945). These two types of Nazi planes made their debuts almost simultaneously.

The first twin jet encounter by an Allied flier occurred July 26, 1944, when a Messerschmitt ME 262 attacked a British Mosquito bomber at 29,000 feet near Munich. The jet flew in above and below

# THE Me-163 JET FIGHTER

## A Comprehensive Report on an Airplane
## Which May Soon Appear in Operations

SIGHTING of five or six Me-163 jet-propelled aircraft on Zwischenahn Airfield (SUMMARY No. 24, *page* 1)—the first time that such unconventionally powered planes have been seen on an operational field—suggests their possible employment in combat in the not-too-distant future.

Previous reports on this aircraft have been issued from time to time, including a brief description and provisional drawing in SUMMARY No. 18 (*pages* 8–9), but AI2(g), Air Ministry, has now prepared a comprehensive paper examining its possibilities more closely and speculating on its tactical employment. The following extracts are from this paper.

**Propulsive System and Fuel Supply :** All the available evidence indicates that the Me-163 is powered by a liquid rocket. This method of propulsion offers several advantages, but suffers from the inherent disadvantage of very high fuel consumption. So great, indeed, are the requirements in this respect that fuel stowage capacity is the determining consideration in the design and performance of a rocket aircraft. From a drawing of the Me-163 based on sketches and reconnaissance photographs, it has been estimated that a space of about 100 cu. ft. might reasonably be devoted to fuel storage.

One of the problems associated with rocket aircraft, where the fuel load must necessarily represent so large a proportion of the all-up weight, is to dispose that load in such a way that there is no appreciable change in the center of gravity as it is consumed. The pronounced sweep-back on the wings of the Me-163, with its consequent effect upon the center of lift, undoubtedly facilitates the disposal of a great weight of fuel in the after part of the fuselage. Having arrived at this stage in the design, it may have been decided to take advantage of the control possibilities afforded by the disposition of the wings to eliminate the conventional tailplane and elevator.

A space of 100 cu. ft. would accommodate about 8,000 pounds of a suitable rocket fuel. It has been stated by Generalmajor Galland of the GAF, during the course of a lecture, that the full throttle endurance of the aircraft is about eight minutes. Since this figure comes from a reliable source and is reasonable for this method of propulsion, it may be accepted as a basis for estimation.

Investigations undertaken in connection with the Hs-293 rocket-propelled glider bomb have shown that the rocket propellant favored by the enemy is almost certainly a concentrated hydrogen peroxide mixed with a small proportion of methyl alcohol, while a potassium permanganate solution fulfils the role of catalyst. On the reasonable assumption that a similar fuel is used for the Me-163 rocket, a specific thrust of the order of 180 lb./lb./sec. might be expected. If 8,000 pounds of fuel suffices for eight minutes, then the maximum thrust developed by the unit on the above basis is approximately 3,000 pounds. This is quite a modest figure for rocket propulsion, and would be readily provided by a small combustion chamber unit occupying very little space.

General Galland spoke of "hot" and "cold" units. The term "cold" might well be applied to a rocket unit utilizing a hydrogen peroxide base fuel with only a small addition of methyl alcohol, since such a unit may operate at a comparatively low temperature. This theory is supported by a statement that the "cold" unit produces a long vaporization trail. The "hot" unit was not ready for operation at the time that General Galland spoke, but this description, coupled with more recent references by prisoners to long flames from the jet orifice, suggests that attempts are being made to improve the overall efficiency by increasing the combustion temperature. This may imply the use of a more concentrated peroxide-methyl-alcohol mixture or some different fuel.

**All-Up Weight :** There have been no direct references in reports to the all-up weight of the aircraft, but deductions may be drawn from certain statements which permit a reasonable approximation. One informant has stated that he has seen Me-163s launched by towing to a height of 10,000 feet, and that the aircraft glided in to land at a very low speed (35 to 40 m.p.h.). Apparently during these flights the propulsive system was not in operation, and it is possible that the observer was witnessing aerodynamic tests of the airframe without armament and with the minimum of equipment. Even so, the very low wing loading which such a landing speed connotes, suggests that every effort has been made to lighten the structure. The weight of the operational aircraft without fuel, however, could hardly be less than, and would probably exceed, 3,000 pounds, and making allowance for the catalyst in addition to the main fuel supply, an all-up weight of 11,500 pounds will be assumed for purposes of estimation.

**Performance :** For the above weight and an approximate gross wing area of 220 sq. ft., the wing loading at take-off would be about 52 pounds. This figure is not so high as to preclude unassisted take-off from a normal runway. On the other hand there is definite photographic evidence to show that, at Peenemünde, experiments have been carried out on a special runway in the form of a shallow furrow, about 1,000 yards long, probably provided with rails (*photo*, SUMMARY No. 19, *pages* 8–9). Such a runway may imply some form of assisted takeoff, possibly utilizing a rocket-propelled trolley, in order to conserve fuel. If special runways of this type prove to be essential to the launching of the aircraft, their appearance on reconnaissance photographs should provide a ready means of identifying those airfields from which the Me-163 is to operate. It is very significant to note that narrow extensions have been made to all the runways at Zwischenahn.

Under the assumed conditions the initial rate of climb with full fuel load would be about 5,000 feet per minute at sea-level, and allowing for compressibility, would attain a value of the order of 10,000 feet per minute at 40,000 feet.

A word of explanation of the marked increase in rate of climb with altitude may not be out of place. Unlike the conventional reciprocating engine and the turbo-jet, the rocket motor will develop its full rated thrust irrespective of speed or altitude. On the other hand, the thrust required to overcome drag falls off as the altitude increases. More important, however, is the rapid diminution in weight resulting from a fuel consumption of 1,000 pounds per minute.

These high rates of climb suggest a steep angle, but contrary to what might be expected, a jet-propelled aircraft does not show to advantage when climbing steeply at a comparatively low air speed. The explanation must be sought in the peculiar property of the jet prime mover that its equivalent horsepower is dependent upon the speed of flight. For example, the equivalent thrust horsepower of a 3,000-pound rocket motor at 250 m.p.h. is 2,000, whereas at 500 m.p.h. it becomes 4,000. To obtain this thrust horsepower with a reciprocating engine and propeller combination, more than 5,000 b.h.p. would be necessary, to double the power of any engine now in service.

The maximum speed of the aircraft is impossible to assess without a much more detailed knowledge of its aerodynamic characteristics than is at present available. Certainly it is in the critical range between 500 and 600 m.p.h. The exact maximum, however, is mainly of academic interest. The aircraft undoubtedly has a substantial margin of speed in hand over anything that is likely to be opposed to it in the near future.

**Tactical Employment :** Obviously the Me-163 would be a very unpleasant antagonist for any reconnaissance aircraft to encounter, and this is a possibility which should be borne in mind. At the same time, it is hardly likely that this would be its sole, or, indeed, its primary, function. It must be assumed, therefore, that its principal purpose is to attack bomber formations and their fighter escorts. That it possesses ample speed goes without saying, but how it will fare from the standpoint of maneuverability is, for the time being, a matter for speculation.

The question of endurance is extremely important in considering its tactical use. At first sight it would appear that, after climbing to an operational height at the expense of, say, half the total fuel load, little could be achieved with the remainder. If the endurance at the operational altitude was only four minutes, very accurate timing and directional control would be necessary to permit of effective interception. On the other hand, in level flight only one-third to one-fourth of the maximum thrust would be necessary to maintain a high flying speed, and if the full thrust were maintained, much of the power would be uselessly expended upon the fringes of the " sonic wall." It is doubtful, however, whether the thrust of a rocket unit can be effectively regulated over any appreciable range, and the possibility of being able to cruise at part " throttle " for, say, 12 to 16 minutes, appears to be remote. Another way in which the endurance might be improved would be to employ the rocket at full thrust in short bursts interspersed with periods of gliding during which the potential and/or kinetic energy thus imparted to the aircraft would be gradually dissipated by the drag.

There is a growing weight of evidence, which cannot be ignored, to show that the latter expedient will be adopted, despite the apparent danger involved in this procedure. In other words, the aircraft will be used primarily as a glider, and the power will be switched on only as necessary to restore altitude or provide rapid acceleration. It has been stated that, by employing these tactics, the aircraft can remain airborne for as long as 2¾ hours. This figure may be rather optimistic, but there is no doubt that, as the weight is progressively reduced and the aircraft more nearly assumes the characteristics of a true glider, it will cruise for a considerable time with only a modest loss of altitude. Here it should be mentioned that, with the fuel expended, the wing loading is only about 14 lb. per sq. ft.

Prisoners have suggested that experience with gliders is desirable or even essential for prospective pilots of the Me-163, and the towed take-off, motorless flights, referred to earlier, may have been primarily intended for pilot training purposes. The possibility cannot be overlooked, however, that with the sacrifice of part of the fuel load so as to bring the wing loading within permissible bounds, the aircraft might be towed up to its operational height and only released when approaching its quarry. It is conceivable that a twin-engined fighter, also destined to take part in the attack, might serve as a tug.

**Armament and Armor :** If it is to be at all effective against fighters or heavily armed and armored day bombers, the Me-163 must carry a reasonable armament comprising certainly two, and probably more, guns of at least 20 mm. caliber.

There have been references to armor and bullet-proof glass, but it seems unlikely that any extensive protection can have been provided in view of the necessity for keeping the landing weight to a minimum. Probably, therefore, the pilot must rely for his safety mainly upon the considerable advantage of superior speed. Even so, the rather corpulent fuselage should provide a good target for hostile gunners, and the fact that in the earlier stages of flight it is largely occupied by fuel would hardly add to the pilot's peace of mind. It must be admitted, however, that little is yet known of the probable effects of various types of projectiles upon tanks containing rocket fuel.

**Drive for Auxiliaries :** With a rocket-propelled aircraft, there is no simple method of driving the various instruments and auxiliaries from the prime mover. This, no doubt, explains the presence of the small windmill at the nose of the Me-163 which probably drives a generator ; the latter, in turn, providing the power for driving the auxiliaries, including the fuel pump. When the aircraft is at rest the necessary current may be drawn for a small storage battery.

**Conclusions :** It seems probable that the Me-163 has now passed the experimental stage, and that it may make an operational appearance at no far distant date. Its performance will undoubtedly be startling, but its very unconventionality prohibits any reliable assessment of its fighting potentialities.

the Mosquito, causing some damage, then pulled away after 15 minutes. Top speed for the ME 262 was 540 mph. By the end of the war Germany had built 1,400 of them.

The second half of the double threat, the ME 163 Komet, was spotted by Allied fighters just two days later, by P-51 Mustangs of the 359th Fighter Group. The rocket engine could boost the Komet's speed up to 600 mph.

Both new planes left heavy contrails and could be observed in the sky initially by this "signature," especially the rocket plane, due to its unusual fuel and the engine characteristics.

In fact it was the scanty supply of the rocket fuel that actually spelled failure for the ME 163 program. Price writes that during September, 1944, the program suffered a disaster "from which it would never recover. In bombing attacks on the towns of Leverkusen and Ludwigshaven that month, two of the main sources of hydrazine hydrate (fuel called C-Staff) suffered serious damage and production was greatly reduced. For the remainder of the war shortages of this chemical fuel would dog the ME 163."

Price adds that a higher priority competitor for the limited fuel supplies was Germany's infamous V-1 "Flying Bomb Program" which used "C-Staff" to power its launching catapults at Peenemunde.

In researching the ME 163, the author attempted to corroborate the ME 163 "kill" described by Pearl, but could not determine exactly when and where the action occurred, even though Pearl's account of the incident more or less fit in with ME 163 flight interception descriptions outlined in the publications provided by Dr. Young and from those obtained from the Maxwell Air Force Base files.

It appears the Komet "kill" credited to Jones and Pearl could have occurred September 12, as indicated by S/Sgt Pearl, or on August 16, a raid in which the two gunners' B-17 had also participated and in which two ME 163s were shot down by bomber gunners—one possibly by Jones and Pearl.

Most Komets were flown from the German rocket base at Peenemunde. Other Komet bases in Germany were located at: Bad Zwischenahn, Wittmundhafen, Stargard, Udetffeld, Brandis, Venlo, Deelen and Husum.

Price noted that on July 28, after P-51 Mustang fighters of the 359th Fighter Group spotted the five Komets over Merseburg, Major General William Kepner, commander of the fighter element of the Eighth Air Force, also issued a message warning of the dangerous new rocket plane.

The Komet had undergone testing as early as April, 1943. The first Komet fighter group became operational in May, 1944—1.JG 400 at Wittmundhafen in Germany—but did not receive its first Komet ME 163B-1a until July—hence the first sighting that month.

Eighth Air Force personnel from the air had observed 1943 testing and described the plane as ."..Small, tailless aircraft, probably jet-propelled, have been seen at Peenemunde on several occasions since April, 1943. Four is the greatest number seen at any one time...will be known as 'Peenemunde 30s'...photographs obtained on September show a 'Peenemunde 30'."

During the ensuing year the plane seen was determined to be the rocket plane called the ME 163.... "obviously the ME-163 would be a very unpleasant antagonist for any reconnaissance aircraft to encounter," stated the publication, "Air Forces in Europe," in April, 1944, three months prior to its initial appearance.

Although Ralph never mentions seeing or firing on either of the new German fighters during his 35 missions, he does mention a buddy downing a twin-jet ME 262 on an August, 1944 mission. It's a ME 163 Komet, however, that the two sergeants are credited with shooting down.

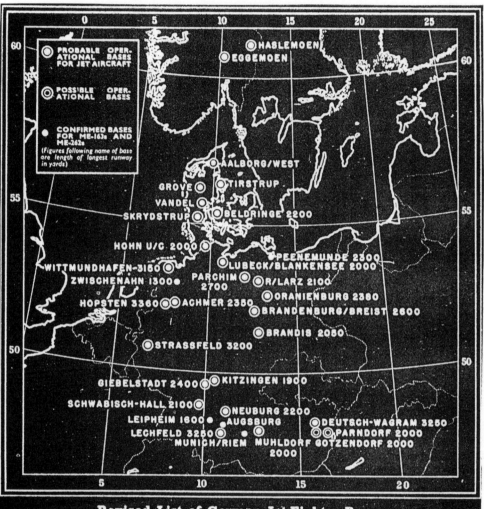

# Revised List of German Jet-Fighter Bases

| Known Bases (Operational or Assembly) | | | | | Possible Bases (Extended Runways) | | | | |
|---|---|---|---|---|---|---|---|---|---|
| Field | | | | Coordinates | Field | | | | Coordinates |
| Augsburg ... | ... | ... | ... | 4820N-1054E | Achmer | ... | ... | ... | 5222N-0755E |
| Giebelstadt... | ... | ... | ... | 4939N-0958E | Brandenburg/Briest | ... | ... | ... | 5226N-1227E |
| Jesau | ... | ... | ... | 5434N-2036E | Deutsch/Wagram ... | ... | ... | ... | 4818N-1637E |
| Kitzingen | ... | ... | ... | 4944N-1012E | Hohn | ... | ... | ... | 5419N-0932E |
| Lechfeld | ... | ... | ... | 4811N-1052E | Hopsten | ... | ... | ... | 5221N-0732E |
| Leipheim | ... | ... | ... | 4826N-1014E | Brandis | ... | ... | ... | 5120N-1239E |
| Munich/Riem | ... | ... | ... | 4808N-1142E | Lübeck/Blankensee | ... | ... | ... | 5348N-1043E |
| Peenemünde | ... | ... | ... | 5410N-1347E | Mühldorf | ... | ... | ... | 4816N-1227E |
| Rechlin/Larz | ... | ... | ... | 5318N-1245E | Neuburg | ... | ... | ... | 4843N-1113E |
| Schwabisch/Hall | ... | ... | ... | 4907N-0947E | Oranienburg | ... | ... | ... | 5244N-1313E |
| Wittmundhafen | ... | ... | ... | 5333N-0739E | Parchim | ... | ... | ... | 5326N-1147E |
| Zwischenahn | ... | ... | ... | 5312N-0759E | Strassfeld | ... | ... | ... | 5042N-0653E |

# JET FIGHTER DEFENSE ZONES

## The Enemy Is Preparing a Line of Bases
## Across Our Bomber Routes into Germany

At least 25 airfields in Central and Northern Europe now seem to be prepared for use by German jet-propelled fighters, and they have been carefully chosen in an attempt to provide protection across American bomber routes into Germany.

It is now apparent that very long runways are required for the operation of both the Me-163 and the Me-262; a minimum of 2,000 yards seems to be essential, and particularly good approaches are also necessary.

These requirements are an important limiting factor in the choice of suitable airfields for jet fighters in a country such as Germany, which has been used comparatively little for basing operational units, and where very little has previously been done to enlarge and improve the GAF stations of pre-1939 vintage. Present development of long runways is therefore of special interest, and can be taken as a useful indication of bases from which the Me-163 and -262 are to operate.

The following airfields in Germany are at present associated with these planes:

| Field | | | | Coordinates |
|---|---|---|---|---|
| Brandenburg/Breist | ... | ... | ... | 5226N-1227E |
| Giebelstadt | ... | ... | ... | 4939N-0958E |
| Lechfeld | ... | ... | ... | 4811N-1052E |
| Leipheim | ... | ... | ... | 4826N-1014E |
| Munich/Riem | ... | ... | ... | 4808N-1142E |
| Oranienburg | ... | ... | ... | 5244N-1313E |
| Parchim | ... | ... | ... | 5326N-1147E |
| Peenemünde | ... | ... | ... | 5410N-1347E |
| Rechlin | ... | ... | ... | 5321N-1244E |
| Rechlin/Larz | ... | ... | ... | 5318N-1245E |
| Schwabisch-Hall | ... | ... | ... | 4907N-0947E |
| Wittmundhafen | ... | ... | ... | 5333N-0739E |
| Zwischenahn | ... | ... | ... | 5312N-0759E |

Five other fields in Germany have been provided with extended runways recently, and while there is no other evidence than this, it may be assumed that Me-163s and -262s may operate from them. They are:

| Hohn | ... | ... | ... | ... | 5419N-0932E |
|---|---|---|---|---|---|
| Hopsten | ... | ... | ... | ... | 5221N-0732E |
| Lübeck/Blankensee | ... | ... | ... | 5348N-1043E |
| Muhldorf | ... | ... | ... | ... | 4816N-1227E |
| Neuburg | ... | ... | ... | ... | 4843N-1113E |

Five fields in Denmark and two in Norway are undergoing similar development. They are:

| Aalborg/West | ... | ... | ... | 5705N-0951E |
|---|---|---|---|---|
| Grove | ... | ... | ... | 5618N-0906E |
| Skrydstrup | ... | ... | ... | 5513N-0916E |
| Vandel | ... | ... | ... | 5541N-0911E |
| Tirstrup | ... | ... | ... | 5618N-1037E |
| Eggemoen | ... | ... | ... | 6012N-1019E |
| Haslemoen | ... | ... | ... | 6038N-1155E |

Possible additions to this list are Gotzendorf and Parndorf Airfields, in the Vienna area, and Beldringe Airfield, in Denmark.

The most striking runway lengths so far observed are at Hopsten, which is 3,360 yards; Lechfeld, 3,250; Parchim, 2,700; and Brandenburg/Breist, 2,600. Work is still in progress on the airfields in Denmark and Norway, where the average length of runways is 2,200 yards.

The location of these bases makes it apparent that the enemy is mainly concerned with forming a line of airfields for the jet-propelled fighters which will attempt to shut the door to bomber forces routed between Holland and Norway. Somewhat less effort has so far been put into the development in South Germany, where the defense is centered on Giebelstadt, Schwabisch-Hall, Neuburg, Lechfeld and Muhldorf, with the possible additions mentioned in the Vienna area.

It is believed that at least four of the airfields in Germany—Munich/Reim, Peenemünde, Rechlin and Zwischenahn—will probably not be used as operational bases, but are mainly concerned with training and development.

Photographs of two of the other fields—Lechfeld and Leipheim—made on 19 July, after they were attacked by Eighth Air Force planes, showed considerable activity. At Lechfeld 22 Me-262s were seen—the greatest number yet found at any airfield—and four Me-163s were also visible. All the planes were dispersed at some distance from the buildings which had been damaged by our attack. At Leipheim at least 12 Me-162s were seen on the field; four or more were outside the so-called "repair hangar," where assembly may have been taking place, and several were probably damaged in the attack. The hangar itself is now badly damaged.

A number of prisoners who have had some experience with the Me-163 and -262 have now been interrogated, and their reports provide some clue as to the GAF's plans for the tactical employment of these planes, as well as to their performance.

**Me-262:** Information on this plane was furnished by a GAF fighter pilot, who had spent three weeks at Lechfeld with a unit engaged in the operational development of the Me-262 and training of pilots to fly the aircraft. Although he had received a large amount of theoretical instruction and had seen demonstrations of the aircraft's capabilities, he had never actually flown it.

There have been several experimental "V" models of the Me-262, and the most recent sub-type which the prisoner saw at Lechfeld in May was the

" V " 8, which he understood had been adopted for series production. He described the belly of the fuselage as being short, the distance between the ground and the lower wing surfaces immediately outboard of the power units as being about one meter (3.28 feet); the power units themselves clear the ground by some 15 inches.

The two main landing wheels of the tricycle undercarriage are housed in the wing section between the fuselage and power units, and when extended, only about two-thirds of the wheel is visible. When retracted, the wheels fold inwards towards the fuselage. All three wheels are fitted with brakes. The wings are of monospar construction, and flaps are installed between the fuselage and the power units; the flaps can only be adjusted to two positions, 20° for takeoff and 40° for landing.

The pilot enters the aircraft by two spring-slotted folding steps on the outboard side of one of the power units and walks over the wings to the cockpit. Provision has been made for installation of a device to eject the pilot automatically with his seat in an emergency.

Each power unit is equipped at its forward end with a small gasoline engine which is used for starting the turbine; according to the prisoner, 10 liters of gasoline (under three gallons) are required for starting purposes, and the small gasoline tank is refilled each time the power units are started. With these starting motors, the shaft speed of the turbines is taken up to 6,000 r.p.m. in two or three minutes, the speed being indicated on a separate rev-counter for each power unit. When proper speed has been reached, the control lever is pushed forward, and the gasoline engines are automatically cut out; the turbine units then begin to operate on diesel oil, and the rate of revolution is increased to 8,000 r.p.m. This is then reduced to 5,000 r.p.m., while the chocks are removed and again increased to 7,000 r.p.m., at which the aircraft begins to move.

During the take-off run, the speed is increased to give 8,000 r.p.m., which is the minimum figure for actual flight. When the power units are started, a long jet of flame exhausts from the discharge conduit, but this flame disappears once the units are running normally. Four fuel tanks supply the power units, and these are placed under and behind the pilot. Fuel is drawn simultaneously from all four tanks to maintain an even trim.

Besides the normal navigational instruments, the panel contains an air-speed indicator calibrated up to approximately 750 m.p.h., an oil gauge, two rev-counters and two dials bearing the overwhelming German nomenclature, *Triebwerküberwachungsgeräte*. This is a power unit control, with one dial for each power unit, and is marked simply with maximum and minimum limits. A pointer moves between these two markings, and it must not pass either marking if the power units are to run satisfactorily. If the pointer falls outside the markings, the aircraft must land immediately. The speed of the turbines is not automatically controlled, but is determined solely by the amount of fuel fed to the power units.

Takeoff speed was described as approximately 150 m.p.h. The plane is airborne after a run of approximately 3,000 feet, and then a speed of 300-350 m.p.h. is quickly attained. The prisoner was instructed that when the aircraft is subsequently put into a climb, the speed should not fall below this figure. Thus the angle of climb is restricted to this minimum speed. The Me-262 is said to be capable of climbing to a height of 30,000 feet in about five minutes.

The speed of the Me-262 at a height of 10,000 feet was given by the prisoner as approximately 400 m.p.h., and at 18,000 feet about 470 m.p.h. He stressed, however, that these speeds were attained with a special test model without armament, and that with a normal operational aircraft, they would be considerably reduced. Strict instructions were given to the trainees that the aircraft was not to be dived at a greater angle than 18°; at this angle of dive, speed would rapidly increase, but the order was that it was on no account to exceed about 680 m.p.h. Landing speed was given at about 155 m.p.h.

The endurance of the Me-262 increases with its height, and the prisoner gave the following figures :

| Height | | | | Endurance |
|---|---|---|---|---|
| 10,000 feet | ... | ... | ... | 45 minutes |
| 18,000 feet | ... | ... | ... | 48 minutes |
| 23,000 feet | ... | ... | ... | 50-51 minutes |

During the period which the prisoner spent with the unit at Lechfeld, a limitation of 30,000 feet was placed on the height to which the Me-262 might be flown ; this was because one of the power units of an aircraft flying at this height had burst.

The prisoner stated that tests on the Me-262 were being carried out by a group of test pilots from the firm of Messerschmitt, who had been assigned to the unit at Lechfeld, and none of the GAF pilots had been allowed to fly the aircraft at the time he was there. A total of some 25 Me-262s at the airfield were being tested to determine their best tactical use.

Although the prisoner had never been told the actual figure of radius of action of the Me-262, he estimated this at about 430 miles at approximately 15,000 feet. He understood the maneuverability of the plane to be below that of a FW-190, which pilots had stated could out-turn it. The general opinion of flying personnel and Messerschmitt engineers was that in attacks on B-17 formations, head-on passes would be ruled out because of the high speed of the Me-262. It was said that attacks would be made from astern, so that the pilot would have an opportunity of firing at least two bursts. It was estimated that the speed of the aircraft would give ample protection from the rear armament of the Fortress.

All of the 25 Me-262s at Lechfeld, although of varying sub-types, had the same armament; this comprised four 30-mm. cannon, two of which were close together in the upper part of the nose and the other two on either side of the fuselage forward of the cockpit and above the wings. The pilot was provided with a Revi sight.

**Me-163 :** A prisoner who had been for five months with Erprobungskommando 16, the experimental unit flying the Me-163, liquid-rocket aircraft, furnished additional information on this plane. But because he had not been closer to it than 300 feet, there is some doubt as to the details he gives on the plane.

The Me-163 is of mixed metal and fabric construction; nose and wingtips are of metal, and the prisoner believed that part of the inboard section of the wings were fabric and wood. The wings themselves, he says, are tapered so sharply as to give a triangular plan view. At the thickest section, they are about 15 inches deep. The rudder is large and has a rectangular appearance. The cockpit merges entirely into the streamlined curve of the fuselage. Its cover was removed to enable the pilot to get in, and then was replaced and screwed down from the outside by ground personnel. The cockpit was not pressurized, and the pilot had a lever by which the cover could be jettisoned in an emergency.

The main fuel tanks are in the fuselage with auxiliary wing tanks feeding into the main tanks. The " A " and " B " versions of the Me-163 were very similar (" A " sub-type is a trainer—" B " is the operational), except that the span of the latter is about three feet greater, the fuselage deeper, and on the nose there are small two-bladed propellers about one foot in diameter, similar to that used for the electric generator of the Junkers W-34.

It is already known that liquid rocket type propulsion is used for the Me-163. Two types of unit are employed, according to the prisoner, the " cold " unit for the trainer version, and the " hot " unit for the operational type. Two substances were used for fuel, known respectively as *T. Stoff* and *Z. Stoff* (propellant and igniter). These names are the same as those used for the two substances used in the Hs-293, but they may be different fuels. The prisoner believed that they differed between the " A " and the " B " versions of the Me-163, because the " A " unit with the " cold " engine emitted a lingering, dirty white smoke trail, while the operational version, or " B " unit, squirted yellow flames tinged with blue for a distance of about 10 feet.

The trainer types of aircraft were fuelled from what appeared to be ordinary tank trucks, while the operational aircraft were always refuelled inside hangars, and no information could be obtained. The power unit of the trainer version started off immediately, but starting the operational Me-163 was a more hazardous proceeding. When everything was ready, the pilot waved bystanders away to a distance of about 50 feet; then there was a buzzing with the emission of a small flame, and after about 30 seconds the large flame developed. The aircraft took off under its own power and was airborne after a run of about 600 yards for the trainer and twice that distance for the operational type. At a height of about 100 feet, the wheels were jettisoned and the aircraft was put into a steep climb.

The training version of the Me-163 was generally thought to have a speed of about 560 m.p.h. The prisoner heard that on one occasion the trainer had beaten the world's record with something approximating 596 m.p.h. The airspeed indicators were calibrated up to approximately 995 m.p.h. The acceleration was very good, and the prisoner stated that the aircraft could change from gliding flight to high speed on full power within about 10 seconds.

The Me-163 trainer had a fuel capacity of 1000-1200 liters (roughly 260-310 gallons), and with this quantity of fuel, it had a full power endurance of about six minutes. Flying time could be stretched by periods of gliding with the power cut off. It was stated that the Me-163 operational version had a fuel capacity of 1,500 liters (390 gallons) and a full power endurance of 10-12 minutes.

One of the Me-163 operational types was fitted with two 30-mm. cannons in the wings. Fitting of other and increased armament was the subject of talk in the unit. Both versions appeared to be equipped with some type of a brake for landing purposes.

The operational tactics and the tactical employment of the Me-163 were still being worked out when the prisoner left the unit, but certain principles had already been determined. The first was that attacks should normally be from astern, and in gliding flight either from above or from below. Head-on attack, as in the case of the Me-262, was not advocated.

When the power was on, the maneuverability of the aircraft diminished; owing to the very limited endurance, it was assumed by the prisoner that the Me-163 would be kept on the ground until the enemy aircraft were overhead, and then take off and use its high rate of climb to effect interception.

## Two Encounters with Jet-Propelled Fighters

Two encounters with jet-propelled fighters have been reported during the past week—one by an RAF Mosquito, which was attacked by a twin-engine aircraft believed to be jet-propelled, and the other by a section of USSTAF VIII Fighter Command P-51s which drove off two Me-163s as they were preparing to attack a combat wing of Eighth Air Force B-17s.

**Me-163 :** These aircraft were seen on the morning of 28 July, near Merseburg. The following account of the encounter is by the leader of the Mustang section :

" The bombers were heading south at 24,000 feet after bombing Merseburg, and we were flying parallel to them about 1,000 yards to the east at 25,000 feet. Someone called in : ' Contrails high at 6 o'clock.' I looked back and saw two contrails at about 32,000 feet about five miles away. I immediately called them to the flight as jet-propelled aircraft. There is no mistaking their contrail—it was white and very dense, as dense as a cumulus cloud and with the same appearance, except that it was elongated. The two contrails I saw were about three-fourths of a mile long, making a 180° turn back toward the bandits.

" It has since turned out in interrogation that there were five Me-163s—one flight of two, which I saw with jets on, and another flight of three without jets. The two I saw made a diving turn to the left, in good close formation, and started a 6 o'clock pass at the bombers. As soon as they turned they cut off their jets.

" We started a head-on overhead pass at them, getting between them and the rear of the bombers. When they were still about 3,000 yards from the bombers they saw us and made a slight turn to the left into us and away from the bombers. Their bank was about 80° in this turn but they only changed course about 20°. They did not attack the bombers. Their rate of roll appeared to be excellent, but the radius of turn was very large. I estimate, conservatively, that they were doing between 500 and 600 m.p.h. Although I had seen them start their dive and watched them throughout their attack, I had no time to get my sights anywhere near them.

" Both ships, still in close formation and without jet propulsion, passed about 1,000 feet under us. I split-essed to try to follow them. As soon as they had passed under us one of them continued on in a 45° dive and the other pulled up into the sun, which was about 50 or 60° above the horizon. I glanced quickly up into the sun but could not see this one. When I looked back at the one which was continuing the dive, approximately a second later, he was about five miles away and down to perhaps 10,000 feet.

" Although I did not see it, the leader of my second flight reports that the plane that pulled up into the sun used his jet in short bursts. The flight leader described it as looking as if he were blowing smoke rings. This ship disappeared and we don't know where he went.

" The aircraft is a beautiful thing in the air. It was camouflaged a rusty brown, similar to some FW-190s, and was highly polished. It looked as though it had been waxed. The published drawing of this aircraft is very accurate.

" Although these two pilots appeared very experienced, they were not aggressive, and apparently were just up on a trial spin."

**Twin-Engine Aircraft :** A preliminary report on the first combat with a jet-propelled enemy fighter has been received from an RAF Mosquito on a photo-reconnaissance flight from a British to an Italian base on 26 July.

At 29,000 feet, near Munich, a probable twin-engine jet plane approached the Mosquito from the north and pulled up over it. It then banked off and made an attack from port from about 800 yards, and another from below, causing some damage to the RAF plane. After about 15 minutes the Mosquito pulled away and lost the enemy fighter.

An Air Force "Summary of Events, Intelligence, 305th Bomb Group, Aug. 15, 1944," Ralph Jones' group, taken from microfilm reports provided by the U.S. Air Force Historical Research Agency, Maxwell Air Force Base, states the foregoing:"Two days later the 305th aided the 40A combat wing which was given the Bohlen Synthetic Oil Plant as the target. The 1,000-pound GP bombs were dropped with fair results in spite of dense smoke over the briefed aiming points. For the first time the group encountered the enemy's jet-propelled aircraft—two ME-163s attacked the high group just after bombs away, severely damaging one of our planes; at interrogation, two crews described this new weapon as resembling a beautifully designed 'Flying Wing' capable of tremendous speed in its attack. A special S-2 report of this encounter was made and subsequently disseminated throughout 1st Bomb Division."

Fuel for the Komet was extremely volatile—80 per cent hydrogen peroxide in water with hydrazine hydrate and methyl alcohol as catalysts. Any leaking fuel could, and often did, burn the pilot's skin and as a result, pilots wore protective gear. A rubberized fuel cell encircled the cockpit on three sides and within the tiny wing. If the fuel catalysts combined anywhere but within the combustion chamber of the rocket motor, the plane would explode.

Descriptions of ME 163 armament differ in various eyewitness reports included in Maxwell Air Force Base information. An October 15, 1944 grouping of fighter and bomber sightings indicated the following:

"It appears from illustrations that two guns probably of 20 or 30 mm. caliber, are mounted in the wing roots. Pilots who have encountered ME 163s have reported that their armor was of at least 20 mm. caliber."

"The enemy aircraft fired one burst from a protruding weapon mounted on its port wing. This weapon, later seen from 50 feet, looked like a single cannon, protruding two feet from the port wing only, none being seen on the starboard wing."

In late July, 1944, a prisoner of the German Air Force reported he observed an ME 163 equipped with two 30 mm cannons in the wings.

As for the ME 163 models, a July 30, 1944 Army Air Forces, United Kingdom Intelligence Summary stated: "The 'A' and 'B' versions of the ME-163 were very similar ('A' sub-type is a trainer-'B' is the operational) except that the span of the latter is about three feet greater and the fuselage deeper....and a hotter fuel was used for the B model."

Those few Eighth Air Force personnel fortunate enough to destroy a Komet by gunfire described the resulting explosion and aftermath as "resembling a large flak burst." S/Sgt Gordon A. Nelson, a 20-year-old top turret gunner in a B-17 named "The Lil Sergeant," described hitting a Komet: "While I had him in my sights, firing, he blew up, like a huge piece of flak exploding. He seemed to disintegrate in mid-air—there was just a big puff of black and he was gone, without a trace."

Nelson was credited with being one of the first to shoot down a ME 163 in a November, 1944 raid over a Merseburg synthetic oil

*PRIOR TO ACTUAL PHOTOS-*
*The twin-engine German Messerschmitt ME 262 twin jet fighter*
*bomber was diagrammed from observer descriptions before actual photos*
*were obtained in 1944*
(AIR FORCE MICROFICHE)

refinery, that place over which Ralph flew four missions and learned to hate.

When taking off, the tiny ME 163's disposable wheels would drop at about 100 feet. The craft landed on an undercarriage skid if it was lucky enough to return to base. Its success in intercepting allied bombers fortunately was limited, partially due to its high speed which was both an advantage and a disadvantage. Its rate of climb was 2.6 minutes to 30,000 feet. The bombers flew at a much slower speed, perhaps 180 to 200 mph.

The Komet often was armed either with single or twin short-range MK 108 3 mm cannons.

Green noted that the chance of a Komet's cannon hitting an Allied bomber "was extremely slender," due, he explained, to an approach speed of almost 600 miles per hour, coupled with the fact the MK 108 cannon fired at a slow speed.

"The minimum distance at which the MK 108 stood any chance of hitting anything was 650 yards to avoid ramming the target. In a rear attack the pilot of the ME-163B had only the time that it took to traverse 450 yards - less than three seconds - to operate his slow firing cannon, and only the combination of expert marksmanship and skillful flying afforded any likelihood of hitting the target," Green wrote.

REPORT BY COLONEL AVELIN P. TACON, JR. ON JETTIES.

I encountered 2 ME-163's fighters over Merseburg at 0946 on 28 July 1944. My eight ship section was furnishing close escort to a CW of B-17's that had just bombed Merseburg. The Bombers were heading south at 24,000 feet and we were flying parallel to them about 1,000 yards to the east at 25,000 feet. Someone called in contrails high at 6 o'clock. I looked back and saw two contrails at about 32,000 feet about 5 miles away. I immediately called them to the flight as jet propelled A/C. There is no mistaking their contrails. It was white and very dense, as dense as a cumulus cloud and had the same appearence except it was elongated. The two contrails I saw were about 3/4 of a mile long. We immediately dropped tanks and turned on gun switches while make a 180 degree turn back twoard the bandits. It has since turned out in interrogation that there were five ME-163's, one flight of two, which I saw with jets on, and another flight of three without jets. The two I saw made a diving turn to the left, in good close formation, and started a six o'clock pass at the bombers. As soon as they turned they cut off their jets. We started a head on overhead pass at them, getting between them and the rear of the bombers. When they were will about 3,000 yards from the bombers they saw us and made a slight turn to the left into us, and away from the bombers. Their bank was about 80 degrees in this turn but they only changed course about 20 degrees. They did not attack the bombers. Their rate of roll appeared to be excellent but radius of turn very large. I estimate, conservatively, they they were doing between 500 and 600 MPH. Although I had seen them start their dive and watched them throughout their attack, I had no time to get my sights anywhere near them. Both ships, still in close formation and without jet propulsion, passed about 1000 feet under us. I split-essed to try and follow them. As soon as they had passed under us one of them continued on in a 40 degree dive and the other pulled up into the sun, which was about 50 or 60 degrees above the horizon. I glanced quickly up into the sun but could not see this one. When I looked back at the one that had continued the dive, approximately a second later, he was about 5 miles away down to perhaps 10,000 feet. Although I did not see it the leader of my second flight reports that the A/C that pulled up into the sun used his jet in short bursts. The flight leader described it as looking like he was blowing smoke rings. This ship disappeared and we don't know where he went.

The A/C is a beautiful thing in the air. It was camouglaged a rusty brown, similar to some of the FW-190's and was highly polished. It looked as though it had been waxed. The published drawing of this A/C is very accurate. Although these two pilots appeared very experienced they were not aggressive and apparently were just up on a trial spin.

Because of the Komet's high speed, and the slow speed of the cannon, most ME 163 bomber attacks were from the rear.

A B-17 bombardier and navigator November 2, 1944, flying the low (C) squadron of the 493rd Bomb Group, attacked by six Komets, reported: "The enemy fired one short burst and one sustained burst of about four seconds. Observer thought there were four machine guns, two in each wing. It was thought that machine guns were employed since the muzzle flash was extremely rapid."

Most USAAF personnel who encountered German Komets report-ed the rocket planes approached with power on, leaving heavy con-trails, but when attacking, their power usually was off with no contrail showing. As one B-17 pilot noted in his report: "All crew members agree that the Komet climbed and dived under power but glided in to attack." And another reported: "The whole time that I was watching, the enemy aircraft (ME 163) never used power after reaching his desired altitude and making his turn on us."

Because of the poor results involving the MK 108 cannon, an alternative was derived for the ME 163B. Dr. Langweiler, the German inventor of the "*Panzerfaust*," a one-man anti-tank weapon, proposed a revolutionary armament which, he claimed, would virtually guaran-tee a Komet pilot a "hit" and probably a "kill" by even the most inex-perienced pilot.

Green, in "*The Warplanes of the Third Reich*," wrote that "Pilots posted from the *Schulstaffeln* to the two operational *Staffeln* of JG 400 had received little gunnery training, and thus possessed virtually no chance of hitting an enemy bomber.

"Dr. Langweiler's weapon, designated 'SG 500 *Jagdfaust*', was just a thin-cased 50mm. high-explosive rocket-propelled shell housed in a vertical tube and fired by means of a light-sensitive cell activated by the shadow of the bomber. Five tubes were installed in each wing, some 30 inches from the fuselage and splayed fanwise, and it was pro-posed that the ME 163B should fly beneath the target bomber at max-imum speed (600 mph), the vertical separation being 65 to 300 feet."

This "*Jagdfaust*" was tested by flying an ME 163B beneath a can-vas target suspended between two balloons with successful results. This was followed by an actual test in combat. Green notes that "Leutnant Fritz Kelb actually destroyed a B-17 Flying Fortress by use of the *Jagdfaust*. It was decided to adopt this new weapon as standard, but only 12 ME 163Bs were modified, and these were too late to join combat."

As for the ME 163's time in the air, flying time could be stretched by periods of gliding with the power cut off. It was stated that the Komet operational fighter had a fuel capacity of 390 gallons and a full-power endurance of 10 to 12 minutes. The ME-163 would be kept on the ground until the enemy aircraft were overhead, and then take off and use its high rate of climb to effect interception.

In recalling the Komet encounter involving he and Ralph, Pearl described the ME 163 as a small craft that flew past their Flying Fortress. He thought the incident occurred during a September 12, 1944 mission to Ruhland, Germany, but he was not positive about the date. Pearl said he was top turret gunner and Ralph was in lower ball. Of course Ralph did not mention any encounter of this type in his entire notebook, including Mission No. 8 over Ruhland. He wrote only that the raid was over another synthetic oil refinery and losses totaled 49 bombers and seven fighters that day.

The following is Sgt. Pearl's recollection of the event 55 years later:

"Deep in Central Germany we flew in high squadron on right (from above). Bombed from 28-29,000 feet to gain some speed. Received a warning (radio) from our area escort fighters, P-51, of enemy jet fighters in the area. Jets and rocket planes made big thick condensation (con) trails. I was at station in top-turret.

"I saw suspicious objects way off at 4 o'clock level. My next look to that region... 'rapidly approaching' I called on my intercom excitedly to Jones. 'Fighters at (now) 5 o'clock level'.

" I commenced firing my two .50 cal guns (not more than 20-40 shots) at the plane now diving below my range-of-fire. Jones picked up on firing at the plane, as it went down. Jones told me that the ME 163 was lifelessly just fluttering down smoking to crash on the ground—non-mountainous. (Ralph's underbelly location was perfect to observe the rocket plane's spiral to the ground).

"To me, the 163 seemed to vibrate as it screamed past and the small wing ripped apart and fluttered as it started down. I can't say on my own that we actually shot it down, but we were given credit for it, and I learned long ago not to question those kinds of things.

"It wasn't an ME 262 jet...it was definitely one of those tiny rocket planes," Pearl emphasized.

In a 493rd Bomb Group report, the speed of the Komet was noted: "The speed of the jet propelled planes was so great and their size was so small, that, as frequently reported in other encounters, the presence of the e/a (enemy aircraft) was known only by the evidence of vapor trails."

One fighter pilot noted: "I estimate conservatively, that they were doing between 500 and 600 mph....the A/C (aircraft) is a beautiful thing in the air. It was camouflaged a rusty brown, similar to some of

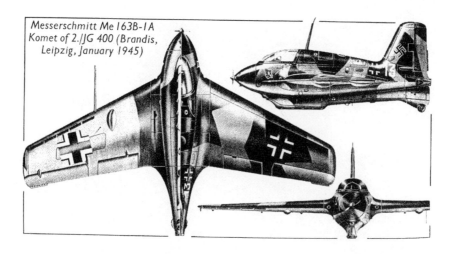

Messerschmitt Me 163B-1A Komet of 2./JG 400 (Brandis, Leipzig, January 1945)

the FW 190s, and was highly polished. It looked as though it had been waxed."

Green states that the German unit flying the ME 163 was *Jagdgeschwader 400, (JG 400),* which lost 14 of the diminutive fighters in aerial combat. Pearl's report indicates he and Jones were responsible for one of those losses.

Morrison, in his book, refers to action by the 305th that day, September 12, 1944:

"The next day, September 12, 888 Fortresses and (B-24) Liberators went to oil targets again (Leuna, Bohlen, Brux, Lutzkendorf, Chemnitz, Ruhland and others that had been attacked the previous day)....JG 400 again put up a sizeable effort as several Komets rose from Brandis. The same frustrating problem with ground vectoring (inaccuracy) placed the majority of the rocket fighters in empty airspace—several groups spotted the Komets but only the 493 and the 94th Bomb Groups sustained attacks.

"At 11:31 a single 163 made a pass on the 94th, coming in from 6 o'clock high, firing cannon, and breaking away to the left. There was no damage done. The 493rd sustained a tail attack by a single 163 but again there were no results. Once again the rocket fighter pilots returned to base with frustration and defeat at the hands of the short sighted improvidence of the Luftwaffe High Command."

It appears the Sept. 12 Komet attack on Jones' and Pearl's Flying Fortress, if it occurred as Pearl recalled, was not included in the official annals of the 305th, not an unusual circumstance, considering the

*PRODUCED 600 MPH SPEED - This is the HWK 509A-2 rocket
engine (rear fuselage detached) that boosted the German
Messerschmitt ME 163B-1 from zero to 600 miles per hour
to an altitude of 30,000 feet in just 2.6 minutes.*
(PHOTO COURTESY OF ALFRED PRICE,
"WARPLANES OF THE THIRD REICH.")

number of aircraft involved in a sortie, but was noted somewhere in the 305th records, since the two gunners were credited with destroying one ME 163. It just may be the credit was recorded on another mission.

In Freeman's book, Appendix E, a section entitled "Daily Losses, T/JS 400 (rocket)—official Luftwaffe figures recorded in the Frieburg Military Archives under *Signatur Rt2/1688*," and for the date of 16 August 1944. is a notation that a single Me 163 was shot down— "Totally Destroyed," as a result of "Enemy Action." It was the second of seven to be lost to Allied action from the period beginning May 22, 1944, through Jan. 20, 1945, according to the Luftwaffe report.

This information differs with that of Price's book. He states two ME 163s were downed that day:

"On 16 August the US Eighth Air Force put up about a thousand bombers to attack a spread of targets in Central Germany, including the oil refinery at Bohlen. Five ME 163s were scrambled, and two were promptly shot down without inflicting any damage on the raiding force."

Price adds: "The Messerschmitt 163 achieved its first aerial victories just a week after that on 24 August. Eight of the small fighters took off from Brandis to engage a force of 185 B-17s running in to attack the refinery at Merseburg. Feldwebel Siegried Schubert carried out a successful interception and shot down two flying Fortresses, other pilots from his unit bringing down two more. That day two ME 163s were damaged, one by return fire from the bombers and the other on landing. It had been a most successful day for the new rocket fighter and seemed to be a portent for its future as a bomber-destroyer."

The ME 163's score of four bombers destroyed that day, however, would mark the high point of its operational career.

Price determined that in aerial combat that 16th day in August, 1944, five Me 163 rocket fighters attacked Allied bombers over Bohlen in Central Germany, and two were shot down without inflicting damage to the bombers. Jones and Pearl were gunners aboard "OH, NATURAL" on that same raid, with Pearl working the top gunner post and Jones in the ball turret. The mission target in Ralph's journal was "Liepzig," but a copy of the 305th Bombardment Group 8th USAAF "WWII Bombing and Leaflet Missions" listed the target as "Bohlen," as did the 305th Bomb Group "Summary of Events, Intelligence," obtained from Maxwell AFB. If Pearl's memory is faulty, this also could have been the mission on which the two gunners downed their Komet. No other mission was scheduled for the 305th that day. Price noted that the Eighth Air Force raid was designed to attack "a spread of targets in Central Germany," and this might have included Liepzig, as Jones noted was his plane's target for that day.

Freeman, in his publication, notes "Official Luftwaffe figures in the Frieburg military archives," the listing for 16 August 1944 is one rocket plane totally destroyed by enemy action, and that as of October 15, 1944, *JG 400* had 51 Me 163B Komets, and that losses up to that date were five shot down by enemy aircraft and destroyed, and four damaged.

Pearl's description of the ME 163 incident included a diagram of the mission in which he noted the 305th Bombardment Group contained 36 bombers in three squadrons of twelve—lead, low and high.

The material obtained from the Air Force Research Center covering August 16 and 24 missions coincides with Price's information about the same two raids:

"...Two days later the 305th furnished the 40A Combat Wing information on the Bohlen Synthetic Oil Plant as the target. The 1,000 lb. Gp bombs were dropped with fair results in spite of dense smoke screen over the briefed aiming points. For the first time the group encountered the enemy's jet-propelled aircraft (in the early days of the ME 262 and ME 163, the word "jet" was often used to describe both jet propelled and rocket propelled aircraft)—two ME 163s attacked the high group just after bombs away, severely damaging one of our planes; at interrogation, two crews described this new weapon as resembling a beautifully designed 'flying wing' capable of tremendous speed in its attacks."

This second report of an encounter with an ME 163 was made August 24 by the 305th:

"On 24 August, flying as the 40A Combat Wing, two groups attacked Merseburg—hits were scored on vital installations to the area. However, losses were high for the 2nd time in August; six planes being shot down. One of the six lost was shot down by another jet-propelled (rocket) plane which attacked the low group north of the target."

Ralph Jones' diary lists very few of his encounters with enemy fighters, whether damaged or shot down. Only on occasion does he note any of his B-17s being hit by fighters; it's usually damage from enemy "flax." We know, however, he engaged Messerschmitt ME 109s, ME 163s, ME 262s, Folke Wolf 190s, ME 110s, and other Nazi fighters intent on shooting down Allied bombers. He fought them constantly, especially in the case of his gun barrel "bending double" during one raid while he was firing at the attackers. As for the others, the reader will have to trust to the recollections of his fellow gunner, T/Sgt. Pearl, (that retired teacher now living in Nantucket) and to Air Force records, as to specific encounters with enemy fighters.

Ralph Jones' widow, Mae Jones, resides in a Stockton, California retirement home. She and Ralph settled in that Central Valley city following his discharge from the Air Force, to assist Ralph's brother, Glen, in the operation of their father's grocery. Later they ran several small restaurants in Stockton until Ralph's death in 1974. Ralph left a son, Mae's step-son, and he also is a resident of Stockton.

Mae kept Ralph's tiny notebook diary, upon which this chronicle is based and she has given her permission for this story.

The little restaurant that Ralph and Mae operated in Stockton, California, called "THE STATE CAFÉ," located at the corner of Park and Grant streets and which boasted a seating capacity of "1000—28 at a time!," still operates at the same location. Only the name has changed. Today it's called "Iris and Louise's."

A photo of the restaurant, as it exists today, is below, and on the following page, is a copy of the menu of Ralph and Mae's State Café shortly after World War II.

# THE STATE CAFE

CORNER OF PARK AND GRANT STREETS

- SEATING CAPACITY -- 1000 -- 28 at a time!
- NO METERS . . . NO PARKING PROBLEMS!
- NO FRILLS . . . JUST GOOD FOOD!

## FEATURING

A COMPLETE MENU Plus Our Renown Special Plate Which Is
Changed Daily For Only

# 95¢

With Soup, Coffee or Tea

Get a Card With Each Dinner . . . . Fifteen of These Cards
Entitles You to a "COMPLETE DINNER ON THE HOUSE ! ! !"

"Homemade Pies Just Like Mother Tried to Bake"

## Our Specialty...Homemade Chili

### MAE & RALPH, Owners

"ALL WE KNOW IS . . . . THE FOOD BUSINESS"

# *Bibliography*

ACTION STATIONS 6. Military Airfields of the Cotswolds and the Central Midlands" by Michael J.F. Bowyer, PSL Patrick Stephens, Cambridge, England

"Bomber Command," The Bomber Command Museum, Royal Air Force Museum, Hendon, England

Department of the Air Force, Historical Research Agency, Maxwell Air Force Base, Alabama - Archives, Microfilm Records, Eighth Air Force, 1943-1944

"Illustrated History of Aircraft," edited by Brendan Gallagher, Longmeadow Press, Norwalk, CT

Information submitted by T/Sgt Charles E. Pearl of Nantucket, MS (an interview)

Information submitted by 2nd Lt. Henry Konysky of Sherman Oaks, CA (an interview)

Information submitted by Dr. Neil Young, Historian, Imperial War Museum, London, England

Information submitted by Mrs. Mae Jones of Stockton, CA, widow of S/Sgt. E.R. (Ralph) Jones (an interview)

Information submitted by Mrs. Henrietta Massie of Jefferson City, MO, widow of World War II Air Force photographer Gerald R. Massie (an interview)

"Mighty Eighth War Manual" by Roger A. Freeman

"Komet; the Messerschmitt ME-163" by Jeffrey L. Ethell

Richard G. Davis, "Air Force Magazine," December 2000 "SPAATZ," Pages 71-72

Richard Hallion, Air Force Magazine, November 2000, "Airpower, From the Ground Up," Page 41

"THE GREAT BOOK OF WORLD WAR II AIRPLANES" (B-17 Flying Fortress), by Roger A. Freeman, Wing and Anchor Press, New York, NY

"The Last Year of the Luftwaffe - May 1944 to May 1945" by Alfred E. Price, Arms and Armour Press, Villers House, London

"THE INCREDIBLE 305TH THE 'CAN DO BOMBERS OF WORLD WAR II'" by Wilbur H. Morrison, Duell, Sloan and Pearce, New York, NY

"WARPLANES of the Third Reich" by William Green

World War II Bombing and Leaflet Missions of the 305th Bombardment Group (H), 8th USAAF, Chelveston Airdrome, England, as compiled by G.B. and Christopher Reynolds

"473 HOURS OF FLYING" - Notebook/Diary of S/Sgt E.R. (Ralph) Jones, USAAF